Amy —

He sets you in the hard place + is always there for you. P in Hope. ♡ Sarah

Ex 14:14

Hope in the Hard Places

Endorsements

"Only a few chapters into Sarah's book *Hope in the Hard Places*, I found hope for some of the hard places I am currently going through. If you're breathing, you have faced, are now facing, or will face 'hard places.' Sarah speaks from experience and writes like a friend walking the journey with you. This is a must-read that will help you not only survive but thrive."

—Ken Davis, Nashville, TN
Speaker, Award-winning author, Trainer in the art and business of public speaking

"*Hope in the Hard Places* is more than an insightful and practical resource book—it gets to the heart of our pain and loss. Sarah connects our story and her story to God's story, and the result is a fresh understanding of the hope found in Christ. This book will be an immense help to anyone facing hard places of any kind."

—Byron Emmert, Minneapolis, MN
Director of Leadership Development, Eagle Brook Church

"What happens when you combine experience, terrific storytelling, encouragement, Bible study, and extremely practical help? You get *Hope in the Hard Places*. If you are experiencing a challenging season—read it. Then share it with someone else. We all need what Sarah has written!"

—Keith Ferrin, Seattle, WA
Author, Speaker, Storyteller

"Sarah Beckman is a caring and compassionate lay minister with experience in the trenches of pain and suffering. As a resident in hard places, she is exceptionally qualified to equip others to find hope there. The very practical help Sarah offers in this book stems from this rare perspective and her combination of experience and compassion."

—Candie Blankman, San Clemente, CA
Pastor of Discipleship and Care, San Clemente Presbyterian Church

"Everyone has felt the panic of inadequacy when that friend or loved one drops a 'crisis bomb' on you. Be it cancer, addiction, divorce or pornography, we all feel helpless, not knowing what to do. *Alongside* by Sarah Beckman is the best resource for comforting and helping those in need around you. *Hope in the Hard Places* meets an important need for the person currently in the midst of a trial. For those who feel alone, this book lights the path out of darkness."

—Ryan Dobson, Colorado Springs, CO
Author, Speaker, Podcaster, Founder of REBEL Rebel Parenting

"When I read or listen to Sarah, I think of the John Mellencamp lyric, 'hurts so good.' Her story, insights, and honesty are simultaneously refreshing and challenging. I was particularly stirred by the concept of taking our pain and offering it up as worship and trusting God to multiply our trials for good and for His glory. I want to be a Job 2:10 and Psalm 126:5 disciple, and Sarah helps point me to Christ for that!"

—Mark Jevert, Kalamazoo, MI
Chief Creative Strategist, NEXT Consulting Services

"Sarah's book *Hope in the Hard Places* offers permission, deep care, and hope for all of us who need to know God is near us in our pain. I felt encouraged, spurred to lament, and know God's gentle grace through Beckman's wise words and Scripture-amplified truths. Go ahead and order *Hope in the Hard Places* and share it like confetti, for us humans traverse hard and desperately need everyday hope for the journey behind, today, and ahead."

—Bekah Jane Pogue, Nashville, TN
Author of *Choosing Real,* Pasture Founder, Spiritual Director in training, Soul Carer, Writer at BekahPogue.com

"*Hope in the Hard Places* is a raw and real, story-driven book that provides practical steps to process, grieve, and stand firm through the test of trials. It gives you permission to grieve, set boundaries, and accept help as you face the most difficult trials in life. Sarah teaches us how to embrace the hard, live in faith, and overcome our fear with hope. You will walk away from this book hopeful and closer to God than ever before."

—Stephanie Porter, Albuquerque, NM
Licensed Marriage and Family Therapist

"*Hope in the Hard Places* is the perfect combination of tough and tender. Being in a hard place is tough, but our tender God sends help through His servants. And even if the worst does happen, you will be okay. In this great truth there is always hope!"

—Elizabeth Murphy, Brookfield, WI
Speaker and Author of *A Roller Coaster, A Roundabout, and A Road Trip*

"*Hope in the Hard Places* is a well-thought-out resource if you are currently suffering or want to prepare for life's trials. Sarah takes you by the hand and thoughtfully suggests ways to navigate life's trials. When you're finished reading, you'll have an achievable plan of action and hope for the future."

—Adina Bailey, Harrisonburg, VA
Co-founder of TakeThemAMeal.com

"*Hope in the Hard Places* brings truly practical advice for surviving the crises that are a part of our journey. No matter what you're facing, strength comes from overcoming discouragement and reaching out for help from friends, family, church, and God. There is hope! So, walk on ... but grab the hand of someone close and walk together."

—Ann Robertson LeBlanc, Norfolk, VA
Vice President, Regent University and Co-founder, Mercy Chefs

"*Hope in the Hard Places* is easy to understand, Biblical, and encouraging. Sarah Beckman offers hope rooted in God's Word to transform chaos into clarity."

—Dustin Woodward, Albuquerque, NM
Pastor, Copper Pointe Church

Hope
in the
Hard Places

how to survive
when your world
feels out of control

sarah beckman

NASHVILLE

NEW YORK • LONDON • MELBOURNE • VANCOUVER

Hope in the Hard Places
how to survive when your world feels out of control

Published in New York, New York, by Morgan James Publishing. Morgan James is a trademark of Morgan James, LLC. www.MorganJamesPublishing.com

ISBN 9781642791037 paperback
ISBN 9781642791044 eBook
Library of Congress Control Number: 2018906012

Cover Design by:
Dawn Sandness
sandness.studios@gmail.com

Interior Design by:
Christopher Kirk
GFSstudio.com

Unless otherwise noted, all Scripture quotations are taken from The Holy Bible, New International Version® NIV® Copyright © 1973, 1978, 1984, 2011 by Biblica, Inc.™ Used by permission. All rights reserved worldwide.

Scripture quotations marked (ESV) are from the ESV® Bible (The Holy Bible, English Standard Version®), copyright © 2001 by Crossway, a publishing ministry of Good News Publishers. Used by permission. All rights reserved.

Scripture quotations marked (NLT) are taken from the Holy Bible, New Living Translation, copyright © 1996, 2004, 2015 by Tyndale House Foundation. Used by permission of Tyndale House Publishers, Inc., Carol Stream, Illinois 60188. All rights reserved.

Scripture quotations marked (MSG) are taken from *THE MESSAGE*, copyright © 1993, 1994, 1995, 1996, 2000, 2001, 2002 by Eugene H. Peterson. Used by permission of NavPress. All rights reserved. Represented by Tyndale House Publishers, Inc.

In an effort to support local communities, raise awareness and funds, Morgan James Publishing donates a percentage of all book sales for the life of each book to Habitat for Humanity Peninsula and Greater Williamsburg.

Get involved today! Visit
www.MorganJamesBuilds.com

In gratitude to my mom,
Catherine Moran.

You taught me how to give—
and to receive.
And to persevere in the hard places.

Table of Contents

Part 3
Journey

Part 4
Destination

Foreword

It was Sunday, four days before Christmas. The sanctuary was magical—brimming with pine-scented garlands, wreaths, candles, and a huge tree filled with twinkling white lights that reflected throughout the room. I paused to breathe it all in. Christmas was everywhere!

Our family of five found our seats as the pianist finished the final carol.

Pastor Dave, using the classic Christmas movie *It's a Wonderful Life* as an illustration, encouraged us to view life through the eyes of faith and gratitude, no matter what our circumstances.

He said, "Even if you have endured, or are enduring, trauma, sorrows, or struggles like depression, abuse, parents' divorce, death of a parent, loss of a child, a life-altering accident, cancer, chronic illness, death of a spouse, or divorce, you still can have a wonderful life."

He continued, "After George Bailey spent time with his guardian angel, Clarence, his circumstances didn't change; his *perspective* did."

Through tear-filled eyes I squeezed my husband's hand, and whispered, "We really do have a wonderful life!" He nodded and smiled back at me.

Kate, our then-teenaged daughter, elbowed me and whispered back, "How can you say that you have a wonderful life when most of the situations Pastor Dave just listed have happened to you?"

Her comment shocked me, but she was right!

With the exception of death of a spouse and divorce, the rest of the list had actually happened to me. How could I still believe I had a wonderful life?

In hushed tones, I replied, "I've learned that even in the toughest times, I can choose how I respond. I can choose hope and to believe God is good even when I don't feel like it's true."

Kate and I later revisited the conversation, and I explained that choosing hope and trusting God doesn't always "fix" things or mean the end of hard times. But, it does bring light—however dim and far off it seems—for the arduous journey.

The reason I believe this to be true: hope and trust usher in the sustaining presence of Jesus, who understands our suffering and carries us through.

If you are anything like me, you've experienced heart-wrenching, "unfixable" seasons of hard. You've likely wondered, "Why is this happening to me?" or "When will this ever end?" Maybe you've wrestled with hopelessness, even invited it in for coffee and a chat, only to discover hopelessness is no friend.

Finding hope in the midst of navigating the hard times is a choice—a difficult, soul- and gut-wrenching choice. But often, we don't know *how* to grasp for hope when we are caught in the undertow of anger, fear, and hopelessness.

And that's why I love Sarah Beckman. Sarah throws us all a life raft in *Hope in the Hard Places* and offers a lifeline for how to choose hope, moment by moment, when life has knocked us for a loop, and we're drowning in sorrow and battling anger and fear.

Her words pierce the raw, hurting places in our hearts. Like a breath of fresh air, hope leaps from the pages and soaks into our sadness. Sarah gently invites us to shift our perspective without clichés, platitudes, or "Bible Band-Aids." And that makes a world of difference.

The reason she is able to speak with authority into our dark places is because she, too, has lived there.

Sarah understands.

In this Instagram, Pinterest-perfect world, where the norm is to hide our pain and only post our highlight reels, Sarah courageously reveals her painful, personal journey with hard times, desperation, and grief.

I love how she shares from her own experience and offers hope, not just theory. She includes practical tools and tips for navigating the hard places in real-time and the challenges of dealing with overwhelming circumstances—and sometimes, overwhelming people.

Sarah reveals how she clung to faith, hope, and love as she struggled to keep her head above water, and how to invite God's light into those dark places. With a tender heart, and without sounding preachy or judgmental, Sarah also dives below the surface to address the difficult questions that, as people of faith, we are often afraid to ask.

In *Hope in the Hard Places,* Sarah shares where to find and cling to hope, how to embrace grace, and ways to ask for what we need when our world falls apart with a phone call, unexpected diagnosis, or devastating news.

As you read, know that it's okay to grieve, struggle, or cry amidst the hard places you're facing. Life is hard, *and* life is wonderful. But keep reading. Know that, in the hardest of times, you have a friend in Sarah, a friend who will come alongside you as you invite hope—and the One who is hope—into your story.

Like George Bailey, we all need a reminder to look at life from a different perspective. And when we do, we are able to find hope in the hard places.

Susie Albert Miller
Author of *Listen, Learn, Love: How to Dramatically Improve Your Relationships in 30 Days or Less!*

Introduction

I've lived through my own dark places. And I've been privy to more tragic stories than I can ever recount to you. Cancer, death, incurable disease, physical and sexual abuse, divorce, aging parents, sick children, infidelity, mental illness, anxiety, depression, bankruptcy, natural disasters—and all the hard situations I haven't consolidated into a compact sentence in a book—are wreaking havoc in people's lives each and every day.

It's heartbreaking.

The truth is, none of us are immune. We can't have enough faith, hope, belief, goodness, obedience, will, trust, confidence, fortitude, perseverance, or prayers to gain a hall pass from the storms of life. We _will_ have hard places. Jesus guarantees it.

In John 16:33 he says, "In this world you will have trouble."

The pain of this world led me to write my first book, *Alongside*, a practical guidebook that teaches people how to love others better through their hard places. As I began to communicate its message at speaking engagements and in the media, people eagerly shared their hard stories with me. I soon discovered that, if you write a book about how to love people in the midst of their pain, the pain follows you.

And all that time, I was unintentionally conducting "research": cataloguing testimonies, finding weaknesses, learning the dialogue of hardship. I discovered that you, the person *in the middle of the trial,* need help, hope, and practical ideas, too.

That's why you're holding *Hope in the Hard Places* right now—because I couldn't leave you out of the equation. I want to show you it's possible to endure, persevere, and maintain your peace and sanity despite the chaos you're facing. And I also want to give you permission to wrestle with your doubts, care for yourself amidst the struggle, and ask for and receive the help you need.

There's nothing more beautiful than someone who's willing to share where they've been. To give hope to the next one who comes along the path. That's why I didn't limit my scope to only what I've experienced. Instead, I interviewed, surveyed, coffee-chatted, phone called, emailed, and otherwise interrogated hundreds of people who've survived their own valleys.

The perspective and experience of people who've "been there" influences these pages. Their voices are present, even if they aren't quoted. Many times, there was solid agreement on the tips, tools, strategies, and truth you are about to read—regardless of the trial.

If you don't share my faith viewpoint, denomination, or beliefs, you can still benefit from the wisdom and resources in this book. Commit to reading these pages with an open mind. Hear the sage advice from seasoned travelers. Listen to their truth. Benefit from their practical ideas. If you do, I know you'll find hope and encouragement to press on even if your world feels out of control right now.

And if your particular brand of hardship isn't addressed, this book will still help you walk your road. Don't fall prey to comparison. Comparing your hardship to another's is never productive. If your weight is different, it doesn't make it less heavy.

Dear sister or brother, I don't take for granted what you are going through. I keep a list pinned to the wall in my office detailing every type of difficulty I could imagine you're facing. I prayed over them and asked God to show me how to minister to you in the middle of it.

I'll never pretend to have all the answers, only to begin the conversation. Your road isn't easy. But it *is* possible to walk it with more insight, dignity, clarity, encouragement, and hope.

I'm certain of it.

Let Psalm 40:1–3 encourage you:

> *I waited patiently for the Lord;*
> *he turned to me and heard my cry.*
> *He lifted me out of the slimy pit,*
> *out of the mud and mire;*
> *he set my feet on a rock*
> *and gave me a firm place to stand.*
> *He put a new song in my mouth,*
> *a hymn of praise to our God.*
> *Many will see and fear the Lord*
> *and put their trust in him.*

One day you, too, will be on the other side. And I can only hope you will speak of God's faithfulness, deliverance, and steadfast love that got you there.

Here's to traveling well. Together.

Part 1:

Terrain

May the God of hope
fill you with all joy
and peace as you trust
in Him, so that you
may overflow with
hope by the power of
the Holy Spirit.

Romans 15:13

CHAPTER 1

Hope

*I will hope continually
and will praise you yet more and more.*

Psalm 71:14 ESV

My first significant hard place was growing up in a family of fourteen children with an alcoholic father. My parents divorced when I was five and my single-parent mom went back to work to support our family. As a young country schoolgirl, I remember waiting in line for food stamps at the massive marble courthouse in the city. I remember how excited we were on the occasions where Great-Aunt Bessie would give Mom a check for back-to-school shopping, so we could get new corduroys from the Gap. When I was sixteen, I remember my brother wrapped the mortgage bill and put it under the Christmas tree for my mom because she had finally improved her credit to the point where she could hold the mortgage in her name.

We certainly didn't have an excess of anything, but we had each other. Family was everything. Those early years of hardship shaped me into an independent, grateful young adult who didn't take much for granted. I learned from the best. My mom always pressed on, even in the direst of straits. She was resilient. And her faith was a firm foundation during those long years of rebuilding.

As an adult, I lost my forty-four-year-old brother to a heart attack. Within two months, I lost a dog and miscarried my second pregnancy with a one-year-old in tow. Whew! Those were some hard days, and I cried in the shower daily for several months.

Fast forward to eleven weeks of bedrest while pregnant with my third child, with a four- and two-year-old on the scene. Then three consecutive back surgeries and a gallbladder/appendix removal within three years—with three kids under the age of eight! During that time, my best friend, Kelley, was diagnosed with leukemia, my dad died, I had surgery for endometriosis, and topped it all off with spinal fusion—my fourth back operation in just six years' time.

I call that our decade of hardship.

Sadly, the list doesn't end there. From losing a best friend, a close neighbor, and a brother-in-law to cancer; confessing an emotional affair to my husband; relocating across the country with three young teenagers; and everything in between and since, life hasn't been a rose garden.

Some of those hardships were before I had a saving faith, and I navigated the terrain differently. But once I knew I could cling to Jesus, I was more surefooted, no matter how much weight I carried.

I can't separate faith from hardship now. I can't face the daily deluge of bad news from people I care about or my own tribulations without looking at it through a lens of faith. I've done it both ways, and I know, beyond a shadow of a doubt, without hope in God I would not be able to stand.

My Hope Comes from God

When my friend Kelley got leukemia, the prognosis was grim. My faith was shaken. The questions were asked and not answered.

She received the news, was hospitalized, and began chemotherapy within hours. It was *that* bad. There wasn't time to do anything but focus on the imminent concerns like her health, kids, husband, and family.

I was tasked with communication and set up a CaringBridge site. CaringBridge (www.caringbridge.com) is designed to keep loved ones informed during a crisis where journal entries and information can be updated as often as needed. Another fabulous feature is a guest book section where people can leave comments and encouragement.

During the initial set-up, I had no idea what to write on it. In hindsight, I should have asked, but Kelley and her family had more pressing matters. So, I just began. I first wrote "Welcome to the page of Hope," which appeared below her name. Then I chose this verse to go below that: "My soul, find rest in God alone; my hope comes from him" (Psalm 62:5).

The introduction said, "This website has been created to keep you updated and to *provide hope* for Kelley and you, her friends, and family."

Somehow, from the start, I sensed that giving hope to Kelley and her family and friends would be integral in this journey. She was diagnosed in 2004 and endured countless treatments and setbacks until her death in 2009. But in spite of it all, she lived well every single day. In fact, she took a mission trip with her kids and a vacation with friends within two months of her death. She never wanted leukemia to take center stage.

Instead, she focused on Christ, family, love, community, strength, and hope. She never wavered.

With her example, and our precious friendship never far from my mind, I want to encourage you—whatever your "hard" is—to carry hope as your constant companion.

Even if we don't get our earthly "happy ending,"
journeying well is imperative.

I love one of the early entries Kelley's husband, Randy, put on the CaringBridge, which is a poignant summary of how we can traverse adversity.

"We do hope to bear witness by traveling our journey with faith, hope, and love. We will certainly fail at times. But ultimately, we hope to reflect the love that we have been given by Him, back to you and this world. Only when we all do this may we truly understand His meaning and message."

All that I've learned in my life to date about suffering and hardship reflects the theme of this book: hope. I can't separate hope and hardship; the result would be too bleak. My mission is to fill these pages not only with hope, but also practical ideas and encouragement for the hard journey you are taking.

And in doing so, may I reflect to you the power, love, and beauty of our One True King who, regardless of what pain or trial we endure on this earth, wins the battle in the end.

CHAPTER 2

Seen

As for me, I will look to the Lord;
I will wait for the God of my salvation;
my God will hear me.

Micah 7:7 ESV

The video text appeared on my phone one Sunday after church. It was a message from my friend, who had lost her husband barely a year before, informing me she had cancer. She wanted to tell me before I heard about it on social media or the CaringBridge site that would launch the next day.

I watched the video and, even though she was filled with hope and certainty that she'd be cured, I fell to my knees weeping on the living room floor.

There are times when it's all too much. There are so many people, like you, who've faced more trial and pain than anyone should ever have to face. I've heard countless tales of wretchedness and heartbreak and hurt. Some days, I hear about people's hard places and I can be strong for them. Other times, like that day, the unfair circumstances of this life slay me.

I was on my knees crying out to the Lord on behalf of my friend for several minutes when this phrase began to replay over and over in my mind. "He will be the lifter of your head." I didn't remember reading it anywhere specifically, nor did I know where in the Bible the phrase came from. It was familiar, yet unknown.

When I was finished lamenting, I picked up my Bible and searched for the verse that contained these words. I found them in Psalm 3:3 NLT, "But you, O Lord, are a shield around me; you are my glory, the one who holds my head high."

I responded to my friend's text message and shared that verse with her. The words stayed with me. For the next several months, the Lord continually brought the phrase to my mind. Simultaneously, another truth wove its way into my thoughts. "He sees you." The two concepts were seamless, as if they'd been written together.

Whenever I shared the message of *Alongside*, I felt like God was asking me to be sure that those in the audience facing great pain and tragedy in their lives received this Word:

 "He sees you in your pain, and He will be your glory, your shield, and the lifter of your head."

You Are Not Alone

Over time Psalm 121:1–2 also added depth to this truth. It reads, "I lift up my eyes to the mountains—where does my help come from? My help comes from the Lord, the Maker of heaven and earth." When we acknowledge God, it can cause us to physically lift up our heads. I see it as God lifting our heads, and when we look to Him and acknowledge His power, we are helped. When we admit how small we are in light of His magnificent creation—the heavens and the earth—the futility of trying to control our circumstances becomes plain. And when can we see the mountain best?

When we're in the valley.

Around this same time, my favorite worship song by Tauren Wells, "Hills and Valleys," was often playing on repeat. The lyrics are powerful. They remind us that we don't get to the mountain alone but in the valleys we should lift our eyes to God who sees us when we are there. The song continues on to remind us that, whether we are on the mountain or in the valley, we aren't alone. If you haven't heard this song, look it up now on the internet and you'll understand for yourself the impact of its beautiful lyrics.

The combination of this song and Psalms 3 and 112 solidified my passion about God seeing us in our lowest place and lifting our heads. Hear this today: when you're walking through the valley, you are not alone.

The God Who Sees

Genesis 16 tells the story of Hagar, the maidservant to Sarah. God promised Sarah and Abraham children, yet Sarah remained barren after many years. She decided to take matters into her own hands by sending Hagar to Abraham so she could carry his offspring in Sarah's place. After Hagar had lain with Abraham, she looked upon Sarah with contempt. Sarah was infuriated and treated Hagar unkindly in return. Hagar fled from her master's home to the desert land.

In the desert, an angel appeared to Hagar. The angel urged Hagar to return to Sarah and submit to her. The angel also told her that God heard her pleas and saw her suffering. He promised Hagar her offspring would be multiplied. Hagar was overwhelmed by the presence of God with her in that desolate, painful place. And she was humbled that He would reveal himself to her. "She answered God by name, praying to the God who spoke to her, 'You're the God who sees me!'" (Genesis 16:13 MSG)

Even though Hagar was used and abused by Sarah and shunned by Abraham, she wasn't abandoned by God. God was faithful.

Dear one, our God sees you in your desert. He knows your pain, He hears your cries for help, and He will never leave you or forsake you. He is the God who meets you in your hard place, who reveals Himself to you. And when it seems like everyone else has forgotten, He sees.

A Stranger

During my errands one day, I popped into a store to check on the possibility of getting an item repaired. I was on the brink of being late to meet someone but, as is typical for me, I was trying to sneak ten pounds into my five-pound sack. (This is one of my weaknesses.) A beautiful sales clerk waited on me. She was immaculately dressed, hair and makeup perfect. Suddenly, I was ashamed of my sweats and ball cap.

She assured me she could help with my repair, so I ran back to my car to grab the item. Since I was in a rush, I handed her my business card, thinking she could get all my information from it and I could dash out to my lunch appointment and only be a few minutes late. But God had other plans.

As she typed all my pertinent information into the computer, she inquired about my first book, *Alongside*, because the title was printed on my business card. I gave her a brief description and she immediately perked up. We engaged in a good ten minutes of conversation as the computer chugged along. I was definitely going to be late to lunch.

We found common ground in our faith and moved on from there. Before long, she disclosed some disturbing, painful information.

"I can't believe that today of all days you'd come in here. I was sexually assaulted over four months ago, and just this morning they assigned someone to my case. I'm in the middle of the mess and here you are, the author of a book about helping people in these kinds of situations!"

She went on to tell me several more intimate and challenging details about her life, including being divorced and raising a special-needs child on her own. Both of us knew it was not a coincidence that I came into her store that particular day.

I felt compelled to pray for her.

As we were saying our goodbyes, I had only a moment to decide whether I'd be brave enough to pray with her in the middle of her workplace. I offered, and she accepted. Right there at the counter, I beseeched the Lord on her behalf. And those familiar words I'd been reciting in my mind over and over again came rushing forth like a tidal wave.

"Lord, You know this precious woman's pain. You know what she's facing and the agony she's endured. But you see her, Lord. You see her and that's why You sent me here today, so she'd know beyond a shadow of a doubt that You are standing with her in the devastation. I am her sign that You see her pain. May You be the lifter of her head. Watch over her, keep her, protect her, and sustain her. Thank You for seeing us, Lord, in the middle of the joy and the middle of the pain. Amen."

With that said, we hugged, and I walked out. I hoped to see her again when I retrieved my repaired item several months later, but she wasn't there. I've not been back, but her struggle remains in my heart.

That beautiful woman inspires me as I write these words to you. Let her inspire you, too—to press on no matter how hard the road gets.

Whatever pain you are going through, whatever struggle you are coming out of, whatever peril you might face in your future, don't ever forget:

He sees you.

He will sustain you.

He is a shield around you.

He is with you in the valley.

And He is the lifter of your head.

CHAPTER 3

Detour

Though He slay me, yet will I hope in Him;
I will surely defend my ways to His face.

Job 13:15

I can't stand detours. There's nothing worse when you're on the road than coming across that dreaded orange and black sign: "Detour." Detours frustrate me because they take precious time and they stand between me and my destination. No one will ever accuse me of having too much patience!

As we travel the road of hardship in our lives, we can also encounter detours. One major detour can take us off the positive highway and send us down the winding lanes of doubt before we know it. If we're not careful, we might never get back on track.

I'm referring to the weighty, miserable, counter-productive detour of "Why?"

A woman once emailed me and said point blank, "I've fallen away from church and I feel like the tumor my daughter has is my punishment."

We can't pretend the Why Detour isn't real. We all want a reason when bad things happen to us or those we love. Our "why" won't go away just because we don't want to talk about it. It's a reality for most of us walking through hard places. Even if it's not always at the center of our thoughts, it's usually hiding somewhere in the back alleys of our mind.

Why?

Why me? Why does my daughter have a brain tumor? Why did I end up divorced when I did everything right? Why did my child die? Why am I sick with this disease? Why is my loved one losing his mind right before my eyes? Why did I get cancer when I eat healthy and take care of my body? Why did I lose my job when the person who never works hard kept hers? Why did my husband leave me for another woman?

Your Why Detour is real.

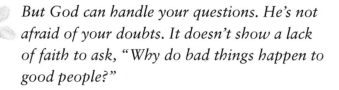

But God can handle your questions. He's not afraid of your doubts. It doesn't show a lack of faith to ask, "Why do bad things happen to good people?"

For the last several decades I've been a student of God's Word and of wise people who teach it. I've learned from Jesus' teachings and tried to apply them to my life. In an attempt to answer this deep, complex theological question, I compiled my personal knowledge, research, and interviews with pastors and faith-filled people I respect. This book includes the best answer I can give you.

If you're still unsatisfied, you don't have to just take it from me; I urge you to study the Bible for yourself. God doesn't want you to be filled with unrest and anxiety about the "why" of your situation. "God is not a God of confusion but of peace" (1 Corinthians 14:33 ESV). He will bring truth when you seek it.

The Big Apple

One of the reasons bad things happen is because good people made a bad choice back in the Garden of Eden. Adam and Eve were created perfect and lived a sinless, idyllic life—until one day they were tempted to eat the fruit of the tree of the knowledge of good and evil. And the moment they tasted that fruit, everything changed.

First, the world went from a perfect state to an imperfect state. Adam and Eve bore the effects of God's curse. (Genesis 3:14–24). Death, trial, affliction, and pain entered the equation and continue to this day.

Second, their disobedience thwarted God's perfect plan for their lives, and they were no longer sinless, but sinful, people (Romans 5:12). At that moment, sin became part of humanity's DNA, woven into the fiber of our beings before we were ever born. We became heirs to this sinful nature that began with Adam and Eve, our spiritual and physical ancestors.

Even if we try to live a blemish-free life, Romans 3:23 says, "All have sinned and fall short of the glory of God." *All of us.* Regardless of race, religion, denomination, socioeconomics, ethnicity, gender, political views, nationality, or any other way we classify people, each of us has sinned.

No one is perfect except Jesus (1 John 3:5).

I once had a conversation with someone who was bent out of shape about this notion of original sin. His contention was, "Why do we all have to be sinful? I'm a good person. I've done lots of good for people and I don't buy that I need God because I'm bad. I'm basically good; just look at my life."

Arrogance and pride blind us if we think we are "good enough." It's impossible not to sin. And the holiness of God demands that sin be paid for, which is why Jesus is the atonement, or payment, for those sins. For all time!

I love how *The Message* puts this concept plainly, "Just as one person did it wrong and got us in all this trouble with sin and death, another person did it right and got us out of it. But more than just getting us out of trouble, he got us into life! One man said no to God and put many people in the wrong; one man said yes to God and put many in the right" (Romans 5:18–19).

Jesus is the only way we can reconcile our wrongs.

So, one answer to the question "Why Me?" is The Big Apple.

Ever since Adam and Eve took that first bite of forbidden fruit, sin has run amok. Evil entered the world at that fated moment in the garden and still pillages lives today. Travesties like illness, disease, murder, theft, abuse, alcoholism, rape, lying, and death happen every day to good people.

We can't deny sin is a root cause of evil in our world. Some trials can be attributed to the blanket of original sin. Others are caused by the sins of others. And some can be consequences we face because of our own personal sin.

Since we've already covered original sin, let's dissect two biblical references that help illuminate how an individual's sin can affect us.

David is one example of his own sin causing personal pain. David sinned big time when he not only slept with Bathsheba, who wasn't his wife, but also got her pregnant, and then had Bathsheba's husband killed to cover up his sin. It was one steaming hot slice of sinful apple pie! Because of David's sin, he suffered three consequences from God: he would never see peace in his house; he was publicly shamed for his private sin; and his son died (2 Samuel 12:10–14).

The notion of our own sin causing us harm is best summarized by this verse: "Do not be deceived: God is not mocked, for whatever one sows, that will he also reap. For the one who sows to his own flesh will from the flesh reap corruption, but the one who sows to the Spirit will from the Spirit reap eternal life" (Galatians 6:7–8 ESV).

Joseph is a biblical example of another person's sin causing personal hardship. When Joseph was serving under Potiphar, his master's wife became interested in him. Joseph was a handsome man, so she continually tried to persuade him to sleep with her. Joseph repeatedly denied her. Finally, he said, "How then can I do this great wickedness and sin against God?" (Genesis 39:9 ESV).

One day, when no one was around, she tried again to get him to acquiesce to her charms and beauty. He ran out of the room, leaving behind his garment. She was offended by his lack of interest in her, so she falsely accused Joseph of trying to sleep with her. Everyone believed her story, and her husband, Potiphar, threw Joseph in jail.

There are times our own sin will land us in a world of hurt, and times when others' sins will do the same. And there are also situations where it's not one person's tangible sin but the collective sin of this world that causes pain, illness, and disease. Sin contributes greatly to suffering and hardship in our lives. It's not an easy "why," but it's true nonetheless.

Little "s"

Little "s" stands for satan. I hate to give him more recognition than he deserves. So, for my purposes, he's getting a little "s," not a big "S"—satan. Either way, satan is capable of many horrific things and is a big contributing factor in our understanding of the "why me" question. Tempting us or others is how he sinks his teeth into us and wrecks our peaceful existence. (Think Big Apple temptations in the garden.)

When we act upon temptations, bad things will happen. We will feel pain or inflict it on those we love.

Temptation results in a myriad of difficulties such as financial hardship, infidelity, divorce, addiction, physical or sexual abuse, unemployment, separation, and others. Some of these hardships can be attributed to our or others' sins as well. But if we are not careful, the dark force of satan at work in our world can take us out.

We are warned about satan's power to destroy in 1 Peter 5:8 (ESV): "Be sober-minded; be watchful. Your adversary the devil prowls around like a roaring lion, seeking someone to devour." He is our true enemy. "The thief comes only to steal and kill and destroy" (John 10:10 ESV).

We see the ravages of satan in the book of Job. Job was upright, righteous, and lacking nothing in God's eyes. But satan didn't believe that Job could still praise God if he lost every praiseworthy thing in his life. So, God allowed satan to test Job. Why?

If we examine the text, we begin to see for ourselves:

> Now there was a day when the sons of God came to present themselves before the Lord, and Satan also came among them. The Lord said to Satan, "From where have you come?" Satan answered the Lord and said, "From going to and fro on the earth, and from walking up and down on it." And the Lord said to Satan, "Have you considered my servant Job, that there is none like him on the earth, a blameless and upright man, who fears God and turns away from evil?" Then Satan answered the Lord and said, "Does Job fear God for no reason? Have you not put a hedge around him and his house and all that he has, on every side? You have blessed the work of his hands, and his possessions have increased in the land. But stretch out your hand and touch all that he has, and he will curse you to your face." And the Lord said to Satan, "Behold, all that he has is in your hand. Only against him

do not stretch out your hand." So Satan went out from the presence of the Lord. (Job 1:6–12 ESV)

God was proud of His servant Job, and He believed Job could withstand the testing of satan and further glorify God, not curse Him. If Job had praised God only because of all that he had, as satan implied, then God couldn't hold him up as "blameless and upright, one who feared God and turned away from evil." Satan took all that Job had—sons and daughters, crops and livestock, property, and even his health. But "in all this Job did not sin with his lips" (Job 2:10 ESV).

The book of Job has forty-two chapters. Throughout, we see Job's struggle, lament, wish for death, questioning, and defense of his belief in God. His wife and his three friends each encourage Job to turn away from God. Job had doubts. Job had struggles. Job had pain. But, in the end, God didn't credit Job's friends with righteousness; He credited Job with righteousness. God said that Job had spoken of Him what is right. (See Job 42:7–8.) God then restored Job's wealth and prosperity to double what he had before.

There is a real battle going on between God and satan. Although satan is an accuser, the father of lies who deceives and schemes to take us out, God wins in the end. In order to stand firm in our faith in the middle of our darkest circumstance, we have to understand this truth. In the meantime, we can also wear the armor of God, which includes the shield of faith to "extinguish all the flaming arrows of the evil one" (Ephesians 6:16).

The Big "S"

If you're still tempted to take the Why Detour, here's another reality to consider. On this side of heaven, there are some questions that won't have answers. We can remind ourselves of our friend Job who tried to understand why. He attempted to explain his suffering, to reconcile it to his behavior or lack of righteousness. But we see that the real answer to why is the Sovereignty of God.

Sovereignty, or the "Big S," can be defined as "supreme power or authority." Because God's Sovereignty is paramount and above all things, for my purposes Sovereignty is getting a capital S.

I love R.C. Sproul's explanation of God's Sovereignty in *Now That's a Good Question*: "If there is any element of the universe that is outside of His authority, then He no longer is God over all. In other words, sovereignty belongs to deity. Sovereignty is a natural attribute of the Creator. God owns what He makes, and He rules what He owns."

God has the ability to intercede on our behalf, but by His authority He also grants each of us free will. This free will can lead to pain of all kinds for many of God's beloved people. And we will never know why or when God chooses to allow suffering or prevent it. That is the definition of Sovereignty: that God alone knows, and we don't.

Susie Albert Miller, a therapist and relationship coach for over thirty years, says it this way: "We want why to be cause and effect. We want a why because then we can fix it or do something about it. But why is sometimes unanswerable. There's a humility to saying we don't know why."

One woman was sexually abused by a family member. As a teenager, she was again sexually abused by a "man of faith." She admits to asking, "Why didn't God stop it?" As she's grown in her faith the woman says, "We don't get to know what God allows or ordains. In His infinite love He gets to decide."

She speaks of how God doesn't love just those of us who are good. He loves all of us, despite our sinful ways. Even if her abusers' free will caused them to sin against her, and even if God didn't choose to intervene, she knows God loves her—and those who harmed her.

This woman is also comforted by God's Sovereign presence, despite her pain. She says, "I know God was present in my pain, and so a part of me was preserved. The part of me that was damaged and broken caused Him to weep. He held my soul, so I could stay sane."

God's ways are higher than our ways. His thoughts are not our thoughts (Isaiah 55:8–9). He accomplishes what He desires and achieves His purposes. There are things we won't understand, answers we won't get this side of heaven. Our job is to embrace the reality of our fallen world, the resultant sin that entangles us, and the Sovereignty of our Creator.

Murder, abuse, abandonment, suicide, depression, cancer, illness, and loss are not God's plan. People may offer you platitudes, or what one friend termed "Bible Band-Aids." It might aggravate you because they've not faced the kind of pain you're enduring. But through it all, God remains Sovereign.

His plan is for good, not harm. And although those plans can be thwarted by satan, sin, and the free will of other people, God doesn't enjoy His children's suffering.

As with many things in life, this isn't a black-and-white answer. There are subtle nuances of faith that make it difficult to put pat answers on complex issues. But God is all powerful, all knowing, and in charge of the overarching plan for this life and the next. And His perfect love can conquer any pain, no matter how monumental. That's not to say He will always change our reality, but He's with us, weeping and mourning and waiting for a day when there will be no more sorrow, no more pain.

When we get off track on the Why Detour, we can return to the route by standing on truth. The truth that the character of God is unchanging. The truth that we love a God who cares for us. The truth that He loves us, He sees us, and He will never forsake us.

We can choose to dwell on our situation and question God's intentions and Sovereign plan for our lives. Or, we can choose to raise our hands in praise to revere His name and presence and Sovereign power over all the earth, despite what has been done to us.

God says of Himself, "Who then is able to stand against me? Who has a claim against me that I must pay? Everything under heaven belongs to me" (Job 41:10–11).

"Why" Is Okay

Before we leave this chapter, I want to be sure you grasp this foundational truth:

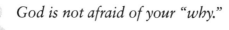

God is not afraid of your "why."

When and if you struggle with the "why," it doesn't make you a bad Christian or person. There is no perfect expectation of how to navigate your trial, and God understands pain and suffering and wondering better than we do!

When Jesus was dying upon the cross he participated in our humanity. Mark 15:34 (ESV) reads, "At the ninth hour Jesus cried with a loud voice … 'My God, my God, why have you forsaken me?'"

We know Jesus lived an unblemished life. If he hadn't, he wouldn't have been able to be the perfect sacrifice for our sins. Yet, in his darkest hour, he asked God, "Why me?" If Jesus asked why, we too can question in the midst of our hard places.

We can come boldly before the throne of grace, without shame. Just because we doubt doesn't mean we don't believe. My friend Susie is a cancer survivor who also struggles with chronic illness. She says sometimes her greatest faith is saying, "Lord, I believe. Help me in my unbelief."

David was the king of lament, expressing his sorrow, fear, doubts, and frustration to God. In fact, over sixty psalms in the Bible are psalms of lament, many written by David. David shows us it's okay to struggle with why. And it's okay to express all of your anger, sorrow, and pain before God in your prayers. Your prayer can be a lament and God can be pleased with that.

When we pour out our hearts before God, no matter what we say, it's a form of worship.

The only way for me to get over something is to say it out loud. Sometimes, I have to say it multiple times. But if I keep it inside, it will eat me alive. The same goes for our anguish. When you express your deepest emotions to God or to safe people—those who will listen and not judge or try to fix your faith—you are working toward getting back on the path of truth. The goal is to not remain stuck in the wilderness of the Why Detour.

Just because we don't feel something in a particular moment doesn't mean our faith foundation is shaken. Sometimes, we need time to catch up. Just like in the psalms, our lament can turn to praise.

When we understand these realities—the forces of sin and satan, the power of our Sovereign God working for our good in the middle of it all, and that God can handle our "why"—we can avoid being completely derailed by the Why Detour.

And get back on track to a journey filled with hope and truth.

CHAPTER 4

Remade

Fear not, for I have redeemed you;
I have called you by name, you are mine.

Isaiah 43:1 ESV

When I was five, my parents got divorced. In the 70s, divorce was far less common than it is today. I think I was the only kid in my first-grade class of thirty-one kids who had divorced parents. I liked being unique, but that wasn't the way I wanted to differentiate myself. Like any other kid, I wished my parents were married, but I didn't focus on it too much.

As the years wore on, I began to compensate for the lack of a dad in my house. I don't blame my mom, or even my dad, but it was a situational factor that affected who I became. There's a theory in psychology called nature versus nurture that always intrigued me. It centers around the question of which aspects of our behavior are inherited at birth or genetic (nature), and which aspects are acquired or learned (nurture). As with most things, there isn't a black-and-white answer. I don't think it's an either/or; I believe it's a combination of the two that makes us who we are and creates certain behaviors.

So where does the matter of faith and God come into play in that nature versus nurture equation? He is in both. God created us, and His hand is upon our nature from birth. But then our upbringing and other people's free will and choices become a part of who we are as well. It's the nurture side of it all.

In my case, I think for a time nurture played a bigger role in my life choices. But then God found a way to redeem the best parts of who He made me to be, despite both my and others' free-will choices.

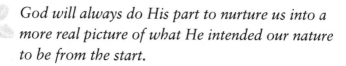

God will always do His part to nurture us into a more real picture of what He intended our nature to be from the start.

I've always sought out strong male influences in my life. Some of my best friends in grade school were two male teachers at the school—Mr. Marousis and Mr. Wagner. I spent hours talking to them at recess instead of playing on the monkey bars with friends. I can picture their faces perfectly in my mind. And I can see their hearts—trying to encourage a "fatherless" wayward girl the best they could.

They were my safe space. They believed in me and, more importantly, they encouraged me.

Another strong male influence was my high school counselor, Mr. Crichton. I'm sure he knew when I wasn't telling the truth. He could probably see right through my façade. But he listened and supported me anyway. And when he had to, he gently called me out. In many ways, he saved my life. We still exchange Christmas cards, and I've thanked him many times. But I think the fact that I'm walking in truth instead of lies is a higher form of gratitude to him.

I was a girl who was always looking for approval. Deep down it was my dad's stamp I sought, but as a struggling alcoholic for most of his life, he was never, ever dependable. And his disease made him less than a great role model. There were days he called me when he'd been drinking—crying, telling me how sorry he was. There were days he promised to be at my basketball game, but never arrived.

When he did show up, no one could miss him. Hands cupped for maximum volume, he'd bellow at the top of his lungs, "Shoot, Sarah. Shoot!" It didn't matter if I was open or if I had the ball. In Dad's estimation, I was the greatest player on the court. He was proud, and generously doled out compliments and affection. But still, his absence always felt bigger than even his larger-than-life presence. And the wounds he dealt were deeper than what could be repaired by the occasional salve he offered.

As a teenager, I wore my self-worth and confidence like a double-edged sword. On the one hand, people couldn't believe how assured and well-adjusted I was despite being known as "the youngest of fourteen kids from a divorced family with a mom who works full-time." On the other hand, I compensated for what was missing in my life and sought worth from people and accomplishments.

High school was fraught with tension trying to maintain people's good impression of me—the confident, smart Sarah who got good grades, played sports, served on student council, attended church, had lots of friends, was a teacher's pet, and loved her family. And the "looking for love in all the wrong places" Sarah, who had sex at a young age, cheated on boyfriends, lied to her mom regularly, partied on the weekends, protected her own interests, and threw her moral compass out the window in exchange for approval or affection every chance she got.

It made for a messy four years.

When I was sixteen, I was at a party and the police busted it. In my attempt to get away, I jumped off the balcony of a second-story apartment and nearly died. The EMT who attended to me at the scene (while my friends hid in the woods nearby) told me I'd be best served if I stopped denying that I was drinking and told the truth because he could smell the alcohol on my breath. I broke my shoulder and the doctor said that if I had been turned just another fourth of an inch, I would have broken my neck and died.

I lived …

And got an underage-drinking ticket.

That EMT was the local Catholic priest who volunteered his time on weekends. His presence felt like divine intervention— another strong male figure who encouraged me and eventually performed my wedding ceremony. God kept showing up even when I didn't fully recognize it.

Why am I sharing all the details of my sordid past with you?

So you can get a clearer view of my present and future: *I'm not who I was.*

A New Identity

My double life has been turned around. It's been a process that's taken twenty-five years, ever since I gave up alcohol and attended AA, married a great man, and found my way to Jesus.

I gained a new identity in Christ.

Ironically, when I was young, impressionable, and striving for love, I was a huge people pleaser. I hated conflict. I didn't want to ruffle feathers. That's one of the reasons I lied to my mom even if it was something innocuous, because I wanted to look better than I was.

Ever been there?

But in 2001, when I had been married just under a decade and had three children under the age of five, Christ got ahold of me and showed me my worth. I received approval from the ultimate

Father. And it wasn't for what I did or didn't do; it was for *who* I was—exactly *as* I was.

The Bible has a verse that sums this up for me: "While we were still sinners, Christ died for us" (Romans 5:8). I'd been trying to get my act together, but I could never keep it together for very long. Perfection eluded me.

> *Human striving will never be enough. It's only a matter of time before something tarnishes our shine.*

But this Jesus I came to know when I was thirty-one years old said I was enough. And for the first time in my life, I didn't have to lie, cheat, or pretend. I didn't need to be perfect; I could be me.

And I was enough.

And once He found me—He gave me a newfound identity. He changed this people pleaser into a woman who could finally speak the truth in love (Ephesians 4:15).

Singular Focus

This call on my life, to speak the truth, has been my greatest blessing—and burden. Many times while writing this book I wanted to give this calling right back to God. I thought, "I'm no one, God. I'm not a pastor. I'm not a counselor. I'm not ordained or educated with a seminary degree. I'm not a doctor or psychiatrist. I'm not even a cancer survivor or parent of a child with special needs. Who am I to write a book about suffering and walking through hard places? Who will even listen?"

And then I heard the voice of my loving, powerful, believing-in-me Father who says, "You could never be qualified enough on your own. I do the qualifying. Your job is to do the truth speaking, and I'll take care of the rest."

I want you to know that I write these pages from a humble and loving place. I don't have all the answers. I've not been through every single thing you've been through. But I've walked in my own hard places, and I'm called by God. That's my credential.

My double life is buried in Christ. All my mistakes, all the pain I caused, all the people I wronged, all the damage I did. And I am made new. Each and every day. Because of the grace of Jesus that makes me clean and worthy (Ephesians 2:8–10).

And my job is to take what the Master has entrusted to me— my pain, hardship, past, and failings, even my successes—and multiply it.

CHAPTER 5

Entrusted

Let the morning bring me word of your unfailing love,
for I have put my trust in you.
Show me the way I should go,
for to you I entrust my life.

Psalm 143:8

The parable of the talents in Matthew 25 is the story of three servants who were each given a sum of money (talents) from their master to hold on to while he went on a journey. It's not clear until he returns, but his expectation was that they would in some way increase what he entrusted to them.

The servant with five talents doubled his, returning ten to the master. The servant with two also doubled his talents and returned four. But unfortunately, the servant with one talent hid it in the ground because he was afraid. When the master returned, that servant returned only the one he'd been given. Nothing more, nothing less. And the master was furious!

Why? Because the master didn't care how it was achieved, but he wanted multiplication. Instead, the third servant was paralyzed by fear and buried his money in the ground. The master said, "You could at least have put it in the bank and gained a bit of interest!"

So how does this apply to the hard thing you're going through in your life?

I pray you will hear me on this.

I believe even our hardest circumstance can somehow be multiplied. Think of faith as small as a mustard seed (Matthew 17:20). Even the smallest, teensiest bit of faith and obedience can be multiplied.

Most of us would wish or pray away our hardship if we could. But we can't always bury our head—or our trial—in the backyard and pretend it's not there. We fear and worry for the future. We want to run and hide and never come out of our room. We don't want to be seen, talked about, or defined by whatever it is that embroils us.

But what if we face it head on, bringing what's in the dark out into the light?

Is there any chance God might be able to help us do some multiplication—even with the worst possible scenario?

In the parable, the master returns to "settle accounts." He wants to know what the servants did with what he entrusted.

In our case, it's not money, but a hardship.

Let that soak in a second.

Now I don't believe that God gives us every hardship we endure in this life. But I know there is good and evil in the world, and *not one of us is immune.* We will have yucky, sinful, tragic circumstances and experiences. Jesus told us so. But he promised to overcome it in the end (John 16:33).

And I am convinced all that we have—good or bad—is entrusted to us.

In his darkest days, when he had lost *everything*, Job said to his wife, "Shall we accept good from God, and not trouble?" (Job 2:10). This is truth, friend.

Whether you want to believe it or not, there is no way we will only get the good stuff in life. And if we get mad or angry at God, then we are the ones who end up losing out. He's the only thing in this life (and the next) that is purely good. If you give up on God because your life isn't perfect, you're the one who will miss out.

We have an opportunity to multiply even the most heinous situations. But it requires putting the master's expectation above our personal comfort (or discomfort).

I know this isn't easy to hear. It isn't easy to write. But I believe it with all my heart. Because I have witnessed what people can do with even the most painful, heartbreaking situations.

They've chosen to multiply instead of bury. And God says, "Well done, good and faithful servant" (Matthew 25:23).

A Few Faithful Servants

I've already introduced you to my friend Kelley. Her greatest testimony in her trial with leukemia was her determined faith and quiet strength. She focused on gratitude, despite her terminal diagnosis and constant pain. For five years, she allowed her faith and life to be on display through her CaringBridge site. It might have been easier to be more private, to not share every hardship with watching eyes. But I know countless people, *who never even met her*, whose faith was increased because of how she trusted God despite her circumstance.

When our dear friends Dan and Pam lost their son, they made a choice to speak the truth about his death. They not only acknowledged his suicide, but also had the pastor declare biblical truth about salvation as it relates to suicide at his funeral.

When my friend Angela's sister died of breast cancer, she decided to run a marathon in her honor and raise money for cancer research to honor her sister's legacy.

My friend Sherrie is a sexual abuse survivor. She is giving voice to the pain of countless women as an advocate and educator about sexual abuse by traveling around the country speaking to students in high schools and universities. (For more information visit: www. couragestartswithyou.com.)

Another survivor lost her rape case in court but chooses to educate students and administrators in high schools about the means and prevalence of sexual abuse in this age demographic in our country.

Patricia P. lost her son in 2004. He was a Navy SEAL killed in the line of duty. I can't imagine the heartbreak a mom would feel losing a young, vibrant son—especially one who was serving his country and pouring out his life to protect innocent people. But she's taken the weight of her grief and placed it on the altar of purpose. She is a Gold Star Mother (www.goldstarmoms.com) and she spends much of her time in service to charities, supporting veterans, and raising money and awareness about these issues.

After the tragic loss of her brother by suicide, Gail began work with professionals to develop a presentation for eighth-grade health classes to teach middle schoolers the truth about depression. They teach the students that depression is a treatable chemical imbalance that shows up on MRIs, not a character weakness. They emphasize that asking for help is the courageous thing to do. Gail also trains other guest speakers on how to share their personal story so that her efforts can be multiplied. The legacy of her brother's death isn't despair; instead, with God's help, it's educating students. If you, or someone you know, have been touched by depression, email Hope-AroundYou@gmail.com to join Gail in this educational calling.

Not every difficulty you face provides a means of public declaration, service, or education. But even a conversation with one person over coffee has a way of multiplying what was once meant for evil but has now been turned into good. And it could be healing in itself.

Psalm 40 is a good place to pause here. If you're experiencing a hard place of any kind, this psalm will be encouraging. I promise.

In the first few verses, David the psalmist praised God for hearing his pleas and pulling him out of his miry pit of pain. He said that God gave him a firm place to stand instead of the muck he was stuck in before. He thanked God for providing redemption and a second chance. He praised God for restoration and healing of whatever ailed him.

But I want to highlight Psalm 40:5 which says, "You have multiplied, O Lord my God, your wondrous deeds and thoughts toward us; none can compare with you! I will proclaim and tell of them, yet they are more than can be told" (ESV). Even though David disappointed, messed up, and sinned against God and others, and faced dire consequences because of it, God still had an abundance of love and grace for him.

 God multiplies His love, even in our pit of despair.

He is the God of multiplication. And He is pleased when we take the trial that's been entrusted to us and multiply it—even the smallest bit. Are you willing to see your present circumstance as an opportunity? As a gift that is expected to be grown, doubled or tripled? It's hard. I know. But when we trust the Master, He will help us do what we cannot do ourselves. His power is made perfect in our weakness. (2 Corinthians 12:9)

Thorns

You might know the story of how Paul ended up in chains in jail for the cause of Christ. But I wonder what would happen if he left that part of his story out? We wouldn't feel quite the same about his credibility as an author talking about suffering if he hadn't suffered himself. We can't separate Paul's tales of heroism in sharing the gospel from the reality that he was beaten, jailed, stoned, chased, and scorned. He is one of the greatest preachers of all time, not to mention a great writer!

But that didn't mean he would have an easy, perfect life. It was his struggle, his pain, his hardship, that makes both those gifts all the greater. Paul was fortified because of what he endured.

If you still doubt, then look at Jesus. What if we took the story of Jesus' life—all his great preaching, his teaching, his miracles, his ability to speak truth and change lives—and removed the hardest part, the suffering and dying on the cross? Would that be a complete picture of Jesus? Absolutely not.

The holy moments at the cross, at the tomb, on the road to Emmaus, and when Jesus appeared to the disciples in the upper room in Jerusalem—what if we left those parts out of the story?

Sure, it would still be amazing, because he saved people's lives every day of his ministry. But without the suffering, without the conquering of the greatest desert journey anyone can face—trial, beatings, being nailed to a cross, rising again, and appearing to believers—you can't comprehend the fullness of Jesus.

You can't leave out the pain and tell a complete story.

His legacy *is* his suffering.

Similarly, if we wish away the parts of our lives that are complicated, painful (figuratively and literally), horrific, treacherous, or gut-wrenchingly hard, we miss out on an important part of our legacy. We miss the holy opportunity to teach more with our lives when it's hard than when it's smooth sailing.

What if we took our pain and offered it up as a means of worship? A time to be in the presence of God, to feel what it was like for Paul, Jesus, or any of our heroes of faith we aspire to be like, and instead rested in it, allowing it to change us.

There are so many Scriptures I could reference here, and if you've suffered for any period of time, you've likely heard them all. But one that was spoken to me when I was in the hospital before my first of four back surgeries deeply resonated.

"I was given a thorn in my flesh, a messenger of Satan, to torment me. Three times I pleaded with the Lord to take it away from me. But he said to me, 'My grace is sufficient for you, for my power is made perfect in weakness.' Therefore I will boast all the more gladly about my weaknesses, so that Christ's power may rest on me. That is why, for Christ's sake, I delight in weaknesses, in insults, in hardships, in persecutions, in difficulties. For when I am weak, then I am strong." (2 Corinthians 12:7–10)

If you've been in a hard place for long, you've likely heard all the phrases:

"Boast in your weakness."
"When you're weak, He is strong."
"Delight in your hardships."
"His grace is sufficient."

Sometimes, you'll want to slap these people for daring to utter what can often feel like churchy Christian platitudes.

But if you pause and reflect, even for a moment, you will see the truth in these words. God's grace *is* sufficient. And take it from me, the queen of self-sufficiency, if we let His power rule in our lives instead, we will be able to boast in our weaknesses!

Still, I resonate with the three times Paul refers to in the passage above. I begged for God to remove my thorn, which was my back pain. I often asked, "God, can't you take away the thorn? After all, everything I do to serve you depends on me being able to *move*, and I can do it far better when I'm not laid up in bed, thank you very much."

And yet, I've endured four back surgeries. Back and leg pain continue to be my constant companions. Ironically enough, my pain is worst when I'm sitting on a plane or at a desk for too long. If the irony is lost on you, let me remind you. I am a writer who sits at a desk for long periods of time writing. And I'm a speaker who sits on planes for long periods of time traveling to speak.

LOL God.

I guess He knows what He's doing, even when I don't understand it. Even though I resist it, even when I wish away my thorns, even when I'd prefer to do things myself, His power *is* made perfect in my weakness.

Blooms

In 2004, I was scheduled to travel from Minnesota to Pennsylvania to preach three weekend services. Back pain wasn't my only thorn; I had just undergone surgery that removed my left ovary and fallopian tube and a procedure for endometriosis on my uterus. It was outpatient surgery, and I expected to be up and running in no time. Only that didn't happen.

As I lay in bed for the two weeks before the trip, I prepared and planned my weekend message, hoping any day I'd wake up feeling full strength. Day five came and went. Day six. Day seven. Day eight. I still didn't feel like I could get on a plane and stand in front of a crowd to preach.

I recall thinking, "God, why did you give me this great message and opportunity, only to pull it out from under me like this?"

It was somewhere in the midst of pain, preparation, and prayer that I heard this word from God, "You can still speak, can't you?

Even if you can't deliver the message in the way you thought, or travel in the style you're accustomed to, you can absolutely still speak this message of truth. Nothing is standing in the way of that."

Fine. (Foot stomp.)

So, I called the church and explained my predicament. I would need assistance with my bag. I would need a wheelchair to take me to and from the gate in the airport. I would need to sit on a stool to preach my sermon. And I would need a lot of grace and provision from the congregation that would welcome me in just six more days.

I was blown away. First of all, the church put me at the top of their prayer list. They sent me a card signed by piles of people in the congregation. They arranged transportation for me and an escort to meet me at baggage claim—wheelchair and all—to pull my bag off the carousel. They tended to my every need, so I never had to stand too long or carry anything heavier than my notes.

I was able to sit on a stool in front of that beautiful church body and present the message God had given me to deliver. I wasn't without pain, and it wasn't a trip that was executed under my own power. Not for a second. But it was one of the greatest lessons I've learned to date about the danger of pride and the beauty of a thorn becoming a blessing.

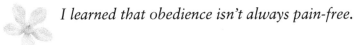 *I learned that obedience isn't always pain-free.*

Paul knew a thing or two. And although his seems like an impossible standard to live up to, we can aspire to be the kind of people who boast in our weakness and park our pride. We need to stop focusing on what we can't do and start to see what we can accomplish through the power and grace of God. We are never so good on our own as we are in the hands of the One who can do all things.

Even if you're struggling to accept this responsibility now, hopefully in the days to come you will be open to this truth. Those of us with thorns understand the beauty of the eventual bloom.

And like a rose that is at the mercy of the sun and rain in order to live up to its full potential, we will eventually boast in the glory of provision. Because I'm telling you, friend, God is ready to show up strong when you feel like you've got nothing left.

Part 2:

Preparation

Let the morning bring me
word of your unfailing love,
for I have put my trust in you.
Show me the way I should go,
for to you I entrust my life.

Psalm 143:8

CHAPTER 6

Packing List

The fruit of the Spirit is love, joy, peace, patience, kindness,
goodness, faithfulness, gentleness, self-control;
against such things there is no law.

Galatians 5:22–23 ESV

I live in what's called the High Desert. We spend our days at an elevation of five thousand feet, but we are also a southwestern state that's hot in the summer. Albuquerque is like a cross section of Phoenix and Denver.

For a midwestern girl, everything is different. I miss grass and water, but there are other attributes to love, especially the three-hundred-plus days of sunshine a year, the gorgeous mountain topography, and stunning sunsets. My new terrain took some getting used to when my family moved from Minnesota, "Land of 10,000 Lakes," to New Mexico in 2012.

The Sandia Mountains are a ten-minute drive from my house and, even though the terrain is beautiful, there isn't a lake to be found for miles. We do have a river slicing our city into east and west portions, but it's not a deep blue, flourishing, swelling river;

it's more of a brown, narrow, not-so-grand segment of the Rio Grande river.

I discovered early on that I had to make a choice about how I was going to live my new life. I could complain and wish away my new scenery, or I could savor its benefits *and* differences.

I said to my friends (perhaps so I would believe it myself), "I'm blooming where I'm planted." That's saying a lot for a place that gets really hot in the summer and doesn't have the trees or flowers to which I'm accustomed.

Because it's so different from where I grew up and spent the previous forty years of my life, I half-jokingly call it our "domestic overseas assignment." These states are as opposite as you can get, even though their initials are barely discernible.

MN and NM. I still write one when I mean to write the other.

But I've come to love the difference. I love how the sun casts a pinkish glow on the mountains at sunset. How the rain is visible from across the city. How the hot air balloons dot the landscape in the peaceful dawn. How the mountain and riverbed façades change with the seasons. How I can see for a hundred miles when I stand on the giant boulders that litter the Sandia Mountains.

Since I've had four back surgeries, I'll never be a runner. Walking is my preferred form of exercise. And in New Mexico, I can walk outside eleven months of the year. But even better, I can hike. There are hiking trails galore. For every ability.

The term "hiker" seemed like it was reserved for the fit young things in the Eddie Bauer, L.L.Bean, or REI catalogs, not for a lake girl like me. But in the years since I switched state codes, I've adjusted to my new terrain. I even trekked the mountain from bottom to top—although it took me seven hours to traverse the nine and a half miles. I'm now a hiker!

I've learned to thrive in this new land.

But it didn't start that way.

The Land I Will Show You

God asked Abraham and Sarah to obey Him and leave all that was familiar. He said, "Go from your country, your people and your father's household to the land I will show you" (Genesis 12:1). It was clear God wanted them to go. "Where" remained unclear. Talk about a hard situation!

I'm not even on the same playing field as these biblical heroes, but I do relate to their plight. When we felt the call to move to New Mexico, fifteen hundred miles away from everything we'd built and established over thirteen years, we felt a bit like Abraham and Sarah.

I remember staring at the familiar street outside our house with tear-filled eyes. How could we leave? Our friends. Our neighborhood. The kids' schools. Our church family. Our extended family. It was excruciating.

Our kids were going into tenth, eighth, and sixth grades at the time, and my husband, Craig, and I uprooted them from every single thing they loved. And moved to a strange, unfamiliar land. Never mind our soon-to-be home state was nicknamed "The Land of Enchantment."

There was very little enchantment in our house in the months before we moved.

People said we were foolish to make our kids switch schools at that age. To leave Craig's safe, secure job and our idyllic life. On paper, they were right. But we knew beyond a shadow of a doubt God was calling us to go.

So, in the summer of 2012, we moved to a hard place. Literally.

New Mexico is filled with dusty ground, boulders, rock landscapes (people call them xeriscapes here, another thing I had to learn), and tumbleweeds that stack up in the cul-de-sac during the windy season like snow drifts in the Midwest.

We also entered a hard place figuratively. We had no friends. And we had to start over in every way. Schools, church, neighborhood, job. Whew! It was rough. There were days I struggled to keep it together. Inevitably, one of the kids would then fall apart, pulling me from the shallow to the deep end of my pool of sorrow.

We spent many Friday nights with only our little family playing games in the backyard. Each person was designated a week to be in charge of what we'd do on our thirty-by-eighty-foot patch of grass with our measly five trees surrounding us. Mind you, we had a literal park adjacent to our backyard in Minnesota. You can imagine how popular Mom and Dad were in these early days.

We definitely lived through a difficult season after that move. Each child took turns being sad, lonely, and disappointed. My husband and I would sit in the hot tub late at night, gazing at the plethora of stars we could see in our new desert night sky, and wonder if we did the right thing.

Sowing in Tears

I love the sentiment in Psalm 126:5: "Those who sow with tears will reap with songs of joy." We cried our share of tears before and after our move. But those same tears watered the soil of our family, producing an abundant harvest. Our situation didn't remain terrible forever. We reaped multiple blessings in the years that followed.

With no one to rely on but each other, our kids forged a bond of friendship that, in some cases, wasn't there before. Our family identity and connection grew stronger. Each of us grew exponentially in our faith between the kids' new school and our new church. The kids faltered, but ultimately grew more confident and self-aware. Our marriage flourished with more quality time alone together. I reevaluated where, when, and how I served the kingdom, and made new space in my life to write. My husband was able to shine more brightly in his workplace than ever before.

It was a hard season, but God was faithful to us in the end.

What Will You Bring?

I chose to pack my bags for Albuquerque with a pile of positivity and hope for our future. I embraced the phrase "Bloom where you're planted" to remind myself to look at the beauty in our new surroundings instead of focusing on what we'd left behind.

When you're navigating a hard place, you too will need to decide what to bring along. This chapter is about identifying the travel essentials you'll need to pack for your journey.

One woman I interviewed in my research for this book experienced a horrific stretch of thirteen months. Her mom had a stroke, her husband was diagnosed with cancer, her dad was injured in an accident, her daughter got divorced, then both her mother-in-law and her dad suffered strokes. A little over a year. Almost every person in her inner circle was either suffering or affected. It's enough to bring a person down.

But her hardship didn't take her out; it brought her to her knees.

She recalls in December, before the first of many trials, the Lord spoke in her prayer time and gave her a theme verse for the upcoming year. In a meeting afterwards, she told her staff about it. The verse was from Nehemiah 8:10, which ends with "The joy of the Lord is your strength."

Nine days later her mom had a massive stroke.

She says, "The Lord dealt with me in advance, preparing me for what was to come. That verse became our mantra. We had to make a conscious decision to choose joy daily." Joy was their anthem, regardless of their circumstance. And the word "Joy" was displayed on everything from coffee mugs to signs, bracelets, backpacks, purses, and any visual reminder they could find. It was all about choosing what lens they would view the hardship through.

Choose a Focal Point

It used to be when a woman gave birth, the staff and doctors would encourage her to bring something to the hospital to focus on during labor. It was called a focal point and was intended to be something that made her feel happy or motivated … or in some way distracted from the pain of childbirth.

The woman who faced more tragedy in thirteen months than most people will in their whole lives chose "Joy" as her focal point. She knew she would need something to get her through. To motivate her not to give up. A truth to fix her eyes upon when she "wanted to curl up in a ball instead."

So just like labor, when you're heading into a hard place (or if you're there already) it's imperative to pack your focal point in your travel bag.

Countless people I interviewed chose a focal point to get them through hard times. My friend Stephanie also focused on "Choose Joy" during thyroid surgery and a cancer scare.

As you know, my friend Kelley chose "Hope." Because we were clinging to hope, we made over three hundred prayer bracelets that people across the country wore as a reminder to pray for Kelley and her family. Each of them had a charm on it that read "Hope." I still wear mine as a reminder that, even though my best friend is no longer here, she left a legacy of hope.

Karen L., who's lived through two separate breast cancer diagnoses and chronic leukemia, chose "Hope" as her theme as well. For a decade, a team of people did a benefit walk for leukemia/lymphoma called Light the Night. The team name was KL

HOPE, honoring both her and our friend Kelley, as both their initials are KL.

Katie and Steve faced his cancer with a focal point of "Immanuel—God is with us." Almost every CaringBridge post or Facebook update they wrote had that phrase included. I was not in the inner circle during his cancer fight, but I still remember that focal point almost a decade later because they used it everywhere.

Susan and Wes had a son born with a rare, life-threatening disease. Before he was ever born, they named him Joshua, which means warrior. They chose a focal point in the form of the hashtag "#bigGodlittlewarrior" and they even got a special onesie and hat made for him with the phrase on it. It's helpful not only for them but also for people coming alongside them. Everyone is aligned in the vision of lifting up their little warrior before our big God in prayer and it keeps the family focused in a positive way.

My friend Michele, when facing down cancer for a third time, chose the phrase "Kick Cancer!" She wore her cowboy boots to treatments and posted pictures on social media of her wearing them in front of the cancer center. A group of women who attended one of her speaking events even had a giant canvas of a cowboy boot made for her, which they all signed.

Kim chose "#cancersucks" as her hashtag and used it on almost every Facebook post. Susie T. chose "Laughter." Angie chose "Gratitude."

Sometimes, your focal point will be a phrase, a whole Bible verse, a hashtag, or just one word. But whatever you choose, it's a great way to set your focus for the hard days ahead.

Here are a few ideas to get you started:

- Be still and know that I am God. (Psalm 46:10)
- Give us this day our daily bread. (Matthew 6:11)

- Bloom where you're planted.
- Kick Cancer's #@$.
- I'm a survivor.
- Hope. (Psalm 62:5)
- Immanuel. (Matthew 1:23)
- Peace. (John 14:27)
- Joy. (Nehemiah 8:10)
- Go God's way! (Proverbs 3:5–6)
- Trust. (Proverbs 3:5)
- I can do all things in Christ's strength. (Philippians 4:13)
- No weapon formed against me shall prosper. (Isaiah 54:17)
- Pray at all times, in all circumstances. (Philippians 4:6)
- His grace is sufficient. (2 Corinthians 12:9)
- Be still. (Exodus 14:14)
- Wait on the Lord. (Psalm 27:14)
- Gratitude. (1 Thessalonians 5:18)
- Rejoice. (Psalm 118:24)
- I'm an overcomer. (Mandisa song, "Overcomer")
- We will not be shaken. (Building 429 song, "We Won't Be Shaken")

There are many more options not listed here. To make your focal point your own, my first suggestion is to open your Bible. I love to use the concordance, that little appendix section in the back of most Bibles where you can look up words (trust, hope, peace, presence, joy, and so on) and then find the corresponding verses. The bigger the concordance, the more options for each word. Then you can spend time poring over all of them to find what speaks to you.

If you don't own a Bible, you can use the online version at biblegateway.com and type in any word in the search bar to help find a focal point.

Establish Your Mindset

It's said that mindset is everything. You would never begin a journey without knowing where you are hoping to end up.

In the same way, when we are in the fray, we need to have a mindset that will withstand the trial.

For the last six summers, I've led mission trips to Haiti. If you've ever traveled to a developing country, you know that things don't always go as planned. One of the things we teach our mission trip participants is the importance of remaining flexible. We remind them repeatedly, "Things will rarely go the way we tell you, so if you are prepared for that, it will be easier to handle when the changes come."

Another charity I volunteer for, Mercy Chefs, provides meals as a form of relief following natural disasters at home and abroad (www.mercychefs.com). They use a flexible Gumby figurine as a mascot in the mobile kitchens. They preach this service beatitude to all their volunteers, "Blessed are the flexible, for they will bend but not break!"

There will always be circumstances out of our control when serving on mission trips or during disasters. That's why this flexible mindset in both situations is essential to the team's success.

When I was put on doctor-prescribed bedrest for eleven weeks with my third child, I was told I could only stand up to bathe every other day. For a time, I bemoaned the fact that I had to take a bath instead of a shower. And then one day I consciously chose to see it as a gift. Before long I'd have three kids instead of two, and then I'd probably give anything for a bath amidst the busyness of parenting. So, I cherished my bath time like I was stockpiling it for later. That simple shift in thinking really helped me get through those days and curbed my complaining.

When my friend Deborah lost her husband, she was determined to stay busy. It was her coping mechanism for working through her grief. She was clear with friends and family that she didn't want to be alone too much. Her mindset, "Stay busy," helped her lay claim to the way she wanted to navigate the hard times.

My friend Bekah, after following God's leading halfway across the country with no job or place to live, daily chooses to live by her family's current mindset, "Trusting scared."

Through chronic illness Susie reminds herself to "cultivate a habit of trust in the Lord."

When Randy and Kelley battled her cancer, one focus was on their family identity: "Team Lewis." It was a way to foster unity and teamwork within their family unit and keep everyone engaged. We still refer to them as Team Lewis to this day!

In the midst of illness of several family members, Ann determined that she would hold fast to the Lord's "diagnosis" instead of the doctors'. I love the mindset that directed her and her family's prayers: "This is not our report!" Whatever projected outcome the medical doctors spoke to them, they determined to "speak life into it."

Ann said, "If you're not at peace, you don't have to accept it! Had I listened to doctors on the first day, I would've given up."

This mindset was critical to her husband's physical and mental health as well. He said, "I would've accepted the whole diagnosis. I was ready to have the doctors do exactly what they wanted. Instead, Ann spoke life when I wouldn't have spoken it for myself.

She wouldn't accept their diagnosis, and her positive voice and mindset brought truth and life to me."

The bottom line is to be intentional, whatever mindset you choose. You can base it on a Bible verse, a significant truth, or even a motivational quotation. Just make it your own and refer to it often.

If you can keep your thoughts framed in the positive, you'll be less likely to get stranded down the dark path of negativity.

Sometimes, there will be a crossover between your focal point and your mindset, but as long as they're both packed in your bag, you'll be ready to tackle the journey ahead.

CHAPTER 7

Team

By yourself you're unprotected.
With a friend you can face the worst.
Can you round up a third?
A three-stranded rope isn't easily snapped.
Ecclesiastes 4:12 MSG

When my doctor advised a second back surgery, only twenty-one months after my first, my husband, Craig, was out of the country. I was in extreme pain, and the more moderate treatment methods didn't provide relief. The doctor said he could perform the surgery the next morning or not for two more weeks. I was in a full panic because I couldn't reach my hubby in the remote French town where he was staying (before we had an international cell phone). I stood in the hallway of the doctor's office in tears, unable to make this monumental decision myself.

So, I called on my orthopedic surgeon friend, who'd been with me since my first back surgery, and he talked me off the ledge. I'll never forget his sage advice, "You can sit around in pain for two more weeks and wait for surgery, or you can begin the healing tomorrow. This way, your pain will be part of the healing and you'll almost be done in two weeks' time! You'll be okay. Even without Craig here."

I had that surgery the next morning as my husband flew over the Atlantic to return home. By the time I was out of recovery he was at the hospital. In that desperate moment, I could have had no one, but I had someone because I'd made my doctor friend a part of my team from the start.

Truth Bomb—Read Before Proceeding

Before I go further, it's important to tell you that you will be best served if you allow others to help you. If you're human, you probably find accepting help from others difficult. But believe me, saying no is not a luxury you have. Before writing this book, I took a survey and asked people who'd been in rough places to offer their advice for others in the same boat.

One woman wisely said, "Accept all offers of help even if you think you don't need it. Don't be too proud to accept help." We'll cover asking for and receiving help in detail in Part 3. I'm preparing you in advance for that discussion—you've been warned! (If you need this advice immediately, head directly to chapter 13 and do not pass go!)

Draft Your Team

Just as focal point and mindset are essential to your journey, so are the people who travel with you. You will benefit from choosing your team of people who will walk with you early on in your crisis. Begin to think about who you know, what abilities, talents, or skill sets they offer, and how they might help you long-term in your situation.

If your hard place is illness of any kind, people in the medical field are good advisors. If you've just lost a loved one, you may need someone who excels at administration or is detail-oriented to help you with arrangements and logistics. Then, while you're grieving, you may need someone with the gifts of encouragement and mercy to walk alongside you. If you're in a sudden crisis, you will want someone with a calm, steady demeanor. If your situation causes financial burden, whether because of a death or mounting bills for any reason, enlist a trusted friend or colleague who excels in the money management area. (I'd need someone for this role, for sure!) If you need help with your children, you'll want a trustworthy, available person who can tend and love them like her own.

When my brother-in-law was diagnosed with melanoma, a couple of dear friends who were both in the medical field were key members of his team. The husband is a doctor and he advised them, explained treatments, and paved the way for care each step of the way. His wife is a nurse, and she made so many things easier with her love, care, and guidance. They were invaluable to both my sister and her husband.

Both my chiropractor and my orthopedic surgeon friend were key players in my decade-long journey of back surgeries. Every time I turned around, someone else was recommending a "magical cure" for my ailments. With the many competing voices, it was their judgment and advice I trusted most, which helped me get through the medical mire I faced for many years.

When Rita faced a future without her husband, an accountant friend stepped in as part of her team. Rita didn't handle the finances for the family, so she was not only grieving, but also overwhelmed by paying bills. She also needed legal advice so a friend from church joined her team.

When Barb lost her husband, her best friend came over once a week for over a year to help her with her finances and the paperwork that has to be handled when a loved one dies. How daunting to do this alone! But she had a cherished, organized friend at her side to walk with her through it.

Relationship Tiers

In *Alongside*, I introduced a concept called the Tier System, by which people could determine the level of relationship they had with someone in order to determine appropriate ways to help someone in crisis. Similarly, as you begin to form your team, it will be helpful for you to assess your relationships in this way. Relationship tiers are a benchmark for what to expect of different people or to determine what's appropriate to ask for or include them in based on your level of relationship. We will refer back to this many times as we go, so mark these pages!

Here are the categories:

Tier 1: Caregiver, close family, close friend.

Tier 2: Friend, family, neighbor, coworker, church member, sports teams, book clubs, small groups, organizations.

Tier 3: Distant family, distant friend, acquaintance, someone you know by association or shared interest.

Tier 4: Infrequent interaction, friend of a friend, you don't know them personally or you've never met in person.

Here's a bit more detail to help you make the distinction:

Tier 1: These are your "people"; you have an intimate relationship and trust them. Tier 1 people can be family, but not every family member automatically belongs here. One clarifying question you can ask is, "How much time do I spend with this person?" For instance, you could have a neighbor whom you see daily, talk to several times a day, and would call first in case of emergency. Just because she's a neighbor doesn't automatically make her a Tier 2. You get to categorize as you like.

Tier 2: You see these people often, but they aren't necessarily your "first-phone-call" people. You know them well, maybe hang out on weekends outside of work, and have lots in common. What you do with them isn't as important as how you feel about them, or the quality of your relationship. Tier 2 people have both a quantity and quality relationship, but since most of us have a fairly small inner circle, this group of people might be larger than Tier 1.

Sometimes, you will even go further in the designation and classify someone as a High 2 or a Low 2. If you are limited in time or margin during your crisis, this additional distinction can prove helpful when drawing the line on things like visitors or access to certain sensitive information.

Tier 3: You might only see these people periodically, like monthly or several times a year. You know them personally, but they aren't people you'd reach out to outside of the associations you share, such as sports, school, or work. If you'd love to see them more often but distance separates you, that doesn't make them an automatic Tier 3 either. If you're not sure, I think quality of relationship trumps the quantity of time you spend with them.

Tier 4: I think of Tier 4 as people you've never met who might hear about your plight and reach out. They may know someone you know but have never met you in person. They could be a perfect stranger, or a friend of someone you know. These are the most distant relationships, and you don't share quantity or quality of time. You get to choose if this person is allowed into your hard place.

1. Know Their Place

Knowing someone's place in your life gives you a solid framework as you make critical decisions. These questions might also be of help:

- Do I consider them a close friend?
- Are they an extended or immediate family member?
- What is their day-to-day context in my life?
- Do I see them regularly?
- Are they part of my church family, small group, or other group I attend?
- Do we have a relationship based on common interest?
- Do they live nearby?
- Do any circumstances make me feel this person is not healthy for me, especially in hardship?
- Do I need to allow this person valuable space or time in my life right now based on our relationship?

The answers to these questions will further help you classify your relationships. These levels are designed to give you a sense of who might be traveling with you in the months and years to come. Further, while some expressions of support are appropriate for Tier 1 or 2, for example, others are less appropriate for Tier 3 or 4.

Relationship tiers will also help you choose people to fill the roles we will describe in the next section. And throughout the book, I will continue to provide guidance about certain situations based on the relationship level you have with people.

2. Find Freedom

Many people find freedom in determining who should and shouldn't be asked or allowed certain access to you during your trial. Let's face it, there are times we don't want to even go to the grocery store, much less have people we hardly know in our house offering to help us. Whether you're grieving a loss, facing a harsh medical reality, dealing with the aftermath of an abusive relationship, or recovering from a divorce, some people are not going to give you what you need.

 Relationship tiers are designed to help you establish healthy boundaries.

You don't have to let a Tier 3 or 4 person clean your house or sort through your family's dirty laundry (unless you want to). This lovely and special honor can be reserved for those amazing Tier 1 and 2 people in your life. You don't have to allow a Tier 3 or 4 person to come over for a two-hour visit or feel obliged to give them the full health (or other) update when you see them at the sporting event for your child.

Likewise, you should not expect a Low Tier 2 or Tier 3 friend to be your everything when you are in need. Certain boundaries are appropriate based on how well you know each other. It's probably not healthy for you to pour out the whole drama of your hardship to a Tier 3 or 4 in the grocery store.

Relationship tiers also provide a way to determine if you've got the people you need to help you through your current situation. I've heard stories of people—like military families, expatriates, or people who move frequently—who have experienced a trial and didn't have any Tier 1 or 2 people in close proximity to help them. If this is you, be willing to seek out someone else. You may need to count on someone who is a Tier 3 in the absence of your tried-and-true Tier 1 and 2 friends.

Maybe you don't feel like you have many close friends. You see other people in the midst of hardship who seem to have throngs of people clamoring to support them. You feel isolated, left out, and alone because you don't have the same kind of support. This is a difficult reality, but if you don't want to go it alone and be miserable, you will need to begin cultivating or restoring some Tier 1 or 2 relationships. It's never too late to make new friends. Also, be open to the potential that a Tier 3 relationship could become a closer friend once you start to invest in them or let them into your hard space.

Designate a Chief

One of the most brilliant ideas I've come across to date is the concept of a "Chief Operating Officer." One family I interviewed designated a friend as their COO when the wife was diagnosed with brain cancer in the midst of her fourth pregnancy. Their COO's responsibility was to manage the needs of the family by coordinating the offers of help, managing requests, organizing resources, and so on. She was the go-to person, and they referred people to her when they offered to help in any way.

A COO's primary mission is to oversee and alleviate undue burden on the person or people in the center of the hardship. If you designate this gatekeeper, it allows you and your family to focus on critical, time-sensitive, or medical-related needs. It's also easier, when people ask how they can help, to refer them to the COO or to the resources already in place to deal with specific needs. The COO could be a family member as well. That's up to you.

Your COO might want to use some of the following resource management tools, or you can put someone else in charge of coordinating these individual efforts. (See specific roles below.) When this person and these systems are in place early on, you will be able to navigate your difficulty without extra baggage on your back, which is the name of the game!

Specific Roles

Alongside also detailed options for specific roles people could assume to alleviate burden in someone's trial. Below are a few roles that are well-suited to Tier 1 and 2 relationships. If no one has offered to help in this way or if people keep asking, "What can I do?" consider asking them to assume one of these positions that suits your needs.

- Chief Operating Officer
- Communications director
- Calendar planner
- Financial advocate/advisor
- Caregiver liaison
- Meal coordinator
- Medical advice collector
- Prayer coordinator
- Transportation coordinator
- Fundraising coordinator
- Paperwork processor
- Legal counsel/advisor
- Hospital helpers

Defining the Roles

While some of the above roles are obvious in their function, I will go into more detail so you have full clarity.

Chief Operating Officer: Manage/oversee all resources, people, tasks, communications, needs, and act as the primary liaison for the family/individual when needed or asked.

Communications director: Manage or set up information dissemination to relatives/large groups/churches/schools/community, through resources like CaringBridge or email updates.

Specific needs/calendar planner: Manage errands, rides, kids' schedules, needs, or tasks for the family/individual.

Caregiver liaison: Manage childcare, post-surgical care, or in-home helpers.

Meal coordinator: Manage offers, delivery, dates, details of meals/food; put systems in place to coordinate between different interest groups that might include church, school, work, clubs, neighborhood, family and/or close friends.

Medical advice collector: Receive and discern any insights, suggestions, offers, treatments, medical or other information that might overwhelm a family/individual; when appropriate, present any useful, necessary information.

Prayer coordinator: Coordinate/plan all things prayer related, including but not limited to prayer meetings, hourly prayer times, specific prayer events such as surgery or key milestones; update prayer chains upon request.

Transportation coordinator: Organize rides to doctor appointments, chemotherapy/radiation, errands, or any other place needed.

Financial director/fundraising: Organize or facilitate fundraising on behalf of individual/family; help with daily financial decisions or details as needed.

Paperwork Processor: Help attend to, consult, or organize paperwork associated with an individual or family's trial.

Legal counsel/advisor: Advise family/individual on legal issues, help fill out paperwork, read documents, or determine next steps; this could be an actual lawyer, or trusted friend who has the ability to understand legal paperwork.

Hospital helper: Stay overnight with you or someone in your family to relieve family members; go to doctor visits; stay on top of paperwork and particular medical treatments; act as advisor or advocate if needed.

With a good handle on the relationship tiers and the roles that people can fill to help you in your hard place, you should be well on your way to lightening your load a bit.

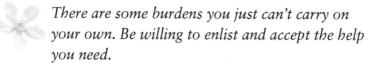

There are some burdens you just can't carry on your own. Be willing to enlist and accept the help you need.

Each member of your team should be chosen carefully. They should be trusted advocates, not bossy bulls. Some team members will need a bit of coaching to align with your vision. And unfortunately, some will even need to be cut from the team if they're not contributing. You don't have to allow people you don't trust to enter into your inner circle, but the people you surround yourself with could be either harmful or helpful.

Choose wisely.

CHAPTER 8

Gear

The heart of man plans his way,
but the Lord establishes his steps.

Proverbs 16:9 ESV

Now that I'm officially a hiker, I've learned never to set out on a hike without preparing. First on my list is getting my backpack ready. My key supplies are always water and food, and if possible, a good trail map. My husband always brings lots of extra gear just to be safe, like rope, a snake-bite kit, toilet paper, a garbage bag, and a flashlight. You never know what will happen and your hike could take longer than you think, so preparation and packing the proper gear is key!

The tools and resources in this chapter will comprise some of the gear you will need for your hike through hardship. They are meant to provide you better footing along the way.

The journey you're facing may feel like an uphill
climb, and some days you will take baby steps.
Other days, giant leaps of faith. But your job is to
get your pack ready and just keep walking.

Trail Head

As we begin, it's helpful to assess your hard place as a whole and to prioritize what needs immediate attention. Crisis in general creates a trickle-down effect, but might involve seeking assistance in any or all of the following areas:

- Food
- Childcare
- Doctor appointments
- Chores/household needs
- Errands
- Finances
- Communication/information dissemination
- Coordination of resources or offers of help
- Housing, temporary or permanent
- Medical care
- Counseling
- Social services
- Vehicle/Transportation

Circle any of the needs from the above list you have now or might have in the future. You will start here when it comes to putting systems or people in place to alleviate your stress and burden. If my list is missing something, maybe it will spark another need you didn't think of yet. Start writing your ideas down so you can track your needs as you go.

In almost every crisis, the first priorities are meals, childcare (if needed), communication, and coordinating multiple offers of help. As for other trials, medical care, housing, counseling, and financial help might be among early considerations.

Many existing tools are available to facilitate meeting these needs, and the time spent setting them up is worth the return in the future.

Existing Resources

Now that you've made a list of what you need for starters, you should ask yourself, "Are there existing resources designed to help me with my specific situation?"

I will provide ideas as a starting point. If you don't find what you're looking for here, it's important you reach out to people in your sphere of influence to ask about getting the help you need. Doctors, counselors, social workers, nurses, morticians, clergy, school administrators and staff, psychologists, psychiatrists, hospital staff, and child-life specialists are just a few of the people who could point you in the right direction. They may also provide the help you need themselves.

Available Resource Options:

- Grocery delivery service
- Church meal ministry
- Church care team
- Church prayer team
- Childcare providers
- Counseling services (church, Christian, or independent)
- Meals on Wheels
- Homeless shelters
- Support groups (cancer, grief, military, abuse, addiction, and so on)
- Alcoholics Anonymous/Al-Anon/Narcotics Anonymous and other recovery groups

- Hotlines (abuse, suicide prevention, prayer, sexual assault, cancer, and so on)
- In-patient treatment centers (addiction, eating disorders, depression/anxiety)
- Hospice providers
- Social services
- Funeral pre-planning services

Thankfully, we live in the age of Google and other search engines. If you are looking for a resource, it can likely be found on the internet by entering a few words in the search bar and clicking go. If you can't find what you're looking for, try getting a recommendation from friends or asking for referrals on Facebook. The collective power of social media is often better than a lengthy internet search.

If a child fails a class without ever seeking help from any teacher or tutor, we would quickly tell them, "There was help available. You only had to take action to get it." The same applies to your particular hardship.

 There are people and resources out there to help you.

If you're going through it, there is a high probability (like 100 percent) you are not alone, and others have experienced similar situations. Seek the help you need so that you don't struggle more than necessary.

Meal, Communication, and Help Management Tools (all free)

There are many outstanding online and other tools designed expressly for the purpose of helping people in their time of need.

From meals to fundraisers, there are a multitude of fabulous tools designed to help you navigate your situation.

CaringBridge (www.caringbridge.org)

Website used for disseminating information to people in acute or long-term situations. It gives you control of what is shared publicly and alleviates the burden of keeping people informed or updated. You give people access to the site and they will receive updates as you post them.

Take Them a Meal (www.takethemameal.com)

A web-based coordination tool for meal management. The service sends email invitations to whomever you designate and reminder emails after they sign up. Allows multiple meal needs on a given day. It also has a blog with helpful tips and offers a meal-shipping service if you don't live nearby.

CareCalendar (www.carecalendar.org)

Web-based system for organizing meals and/or other help. It allows creation of a personalized calendar for those in need, including meals, driving, errands, childcare, cleaning, rides, and yard work. One-stop shop to coordinate help and allows for journal updates as well.

Lotsa Helping Hands (www.lotsahelpinghands.com)

Website for coordinating meals or other help. Best suited for large communities, offers open or closed status. Includes message boards, events, tasks, visits, and errands.

SignUpGenius (www.signupgenius.com)

An online software tool for volunteer management and event planning. Best used for a single event, like a funeral or fundraiser, or a repeated larger event.

Financial Tools

One popular and beneficial way to relieve financial burden during a crisis or to help with medical bills is to solicit donations through a web-based program. Often these campaigns or fundraising efforts are shared with friends and family through social media or email. While not everyone is comfortable asking for help in such a public fashion, you can't underestimate the power of many. When it works, it works! Be aware that some of these platforms take a percentage of what you raise, but lots of people feel more comfortable donating in this more secure way.

Online fundraising platforms:

GoFundMe (www.gofundme.com)

YouCaring (www.youcaring.com)

CrowdRise (www.crowdrise.com)

Fundly (www.fundly.com)

Money management/debt reduction courses

If you're looking for help with debt, money management, or recovering from a rough financial past, there are many educational and practical options available.

Crown Financial's "MoneyLife" (www.crown.org/personal-finance/)

Dave Ramsey's "Financial Peace University" (www.daveramsey.com/fpu/)

Finicity's "Mvelopes" Budget System (www.mvelopes.com)

Financial Insights

Carrie and Kassandra, coming from completely different hard places, both benefitted from Dave Ramsey's Financial Peace University. When Carrie was diagnosed with breast cancer, she met her out of pocket insurance maximum with one week left in the calendar year. This meant her deductible and out of pocket maximum were both reset before she realized any benefit. Because of this, her medical bills were exorbitant. At one point she remembers posting on Facebook that she had a total of $67,000 in current bills.

How did she manage as a divorced, single mom? She said she'd learned the principle in Dave Ramsey's course about the debt snowball. The premise is to take the smallest debt first and pay it off. Then keep working through the list. Additionally, she went to all the creditors and got on a payment plan. She opted for the lowest amount they would accept, even if she could pay more. That way she was making progress in the right direction, instead of ignoring the bills and adding anxiety about paying them all. She said, "I asked, and they helped."

Kassandra's experience was similar. In the middle of their huge legal battle, she and her husband felt called to take Financial Peace University. She says, "We had to be intentional about looking at our finances and be open to learning a new way to see things. That class showed us it was possible to pay for our mounting debt and that we weren't as bad off as we thought." They itemized everything they owed and started to pay things off systematically.

Tiffany's daughter was born with a severe medical condition. When her daughter was around a year old, Tiffany got divorced. To get through her financial hardship, she first applied for disability. She also enlisted outside help from the social worker at the hospital who helped her apply for Medicaid. She said qualifying for disability was a huge challenge. Her advice: "They almost always deny your first request. Be persistent. You have to be willing to continue to fight for what you need."

Surviving your trial, like hiking, requires planning. We have to consult the map, plot our course, prepare our minds, and pack our gear. No matter if it's a short one-mile hike or a weeklong expedition, taking time to put key resources and people in place will help you better face what lies ahead.

Do your best to account for what you think you need and work toward solutions when possible. But remember to lean on God and trust Him to establish His purpose in the midst of your plans.

CHAPTER 9

First Aid

He gives power to the faint,
and to him who has no might He increases strength.
Isaiah 40:29 ESV

When I was pregnant with my third child, we had just moved to a new state. So, I had to find a new OB/GYN. Initially, I chose a practice that accepted my insurance and a doctor who had an opening. After my first appointment, I was less than thrilled with his bedside manner and our lack of connection. Yet I agonized over switching because I didn't want to make him feel badly. I guess I still wrestled with the beast of my people pleasing nature.

After laboring over the decision with my husband and others, I bravely called the office and asked if there might be another doctor I could see. They offered a new option: Dr. Donna Block. Moments into my first visit with her I knew I'd made the perfect choice. She was kind, gentle, smart, engaging, and encouraging, and she completely set me at ease.

Little did I know how essential that decision would be when months later I began preterm labor when I was twenty-seven weeks pregnant. I remember the moment in the hospital when she broke the news to me that I wouldn't be leaving for vacation to Mexico in a few days with my hubby and our then four- and two-year-olds. Instead, I'd be headed to a "vacation" in my bedroom for the next eleven weeks!

This devastating news was only the beginning. I feared for our baby's health and worried if the medication and prescribed bedrest would be enough to keep labor at bay for three more months. But instead of being anxious about my doctor and our relationship, I felt assured in the trusted hands of Dr. Block. I was confident in her decisions and every detail of how she handled my care. Her calm, assured demeanor was balm to my soul.

My daughter was born healthy at over thirty-nine weeks, and Dr. Block continued to be my doctor for a decade or more afterward. I'm so glad I took the initiative to change my doctor when I didn't feel comfortable.

You're the Customer

I've witnessed countless people who don't take initiative with their own health and comfort with their care provider. I've heard tragic stories about people who begged their doctors to pursue a diagnosis and were unsatisfied, with either a lack of action or an ambivalent response.

Many doctors are amazing and wonderful and will be the perfect choice for you. But I want to be clear that you are the customer, and it's up to you to be confident and comfortable with your practitioner. You are a paying client, and should be satisfied with every aspect of your care. If you need to change doctors, do so!

Additionally, you should never feel guilty about getting a second opinion. It's common practice, and any reasonable, professional doctor would not deny you that opportunity. I've been through this myself and almost allowed my concern over hurting someone's feelings to prevail over my best judgment when it came to a second opinion. Before undergoing my fourth back surgery in six years' time, I solicited a second opinion from a different doctor than the one who was recommending I have another surgery.

Although it was extremely difficult for me to call and request that my MRI results be sent somewhere else, I was determined to do the right thing for me and my family and not make it personal. The two doctors' opinions differed greatly, so in the end it was up to me to decide. I followed the advice of my original doctor but felt much more informed about all the advantages and disadvantages of both options when making my choice.

Don't Give Up

My chiropractor is involved with a charity benefitting Parkinson's disease. As such, he's well versed in how its signs and symptoms manifest themselves in patients. He was treating a patient for neck and back pain when she told him she had been diagnosed with Parkinson's ten years prior. He asked her if she was responsive to the medications. She told him she'd never had any relief or help from the medications. He was perplexed because he didn't recognize classic symptoms in her demeanor and recommended she ask her doctor to repeat her blood work and tests.

She returned to the chiropractor's office and reported that her neurologist was offended and unwilling to repeat the tests on the advice of a chiropractor. The chiropractor recommended she fire her doctor and find someone else who'd perform the tests. Although she was reluctant, she couldn't argue with the fact that for a decade she'd had no relief of her "symptoms." Eventually, she found a new doctor and had her tests repeated. She did not have Parkinson's after all. But now she was dealing with the aftereffects of taking an unnecessary medication for ten years.

People make mistakes. That is human nature. But if you feel like you aren't getting what you need, or don't feel content with a diagnosis, you are entitled to either a new doctor or a second opinion. Be bold and brave, and advocate for yourself when you know something's not right.

 Don't let anyone make you feel less than. You are worthy of the best medical care possible.

Fight for the best you can get, knowing your health is at stake. And don't give up if you know something's not right.

Some advice for navigating the medical mire:

- Ask your health professionals lots of questions.
- Keep a detailed journal of issues or health history.
- Create a three-ring binder for questions and to track treatment recommendations.
- Be concise in asking questions.
- Rely on past experience, if applicable.
- Don't search the internet too much. Use only trusted websites, like the Mayo Clinic.
- Keep trying different routes to help.
- Have a friend or family member do medical research.
- Be open to suggestions, but don't feel obliged.
- Use a medical advice collector.
- Bring the same person to every appointment so there is another consistent set of ears.

Handling Medical Advice

One of the hardest things to figure out is how to process and handle all the medical advice you'll receive. (Actually, no matter what your hard place is, people will want to give you advice. So even if your issue isn't medical, you can pay attention here too.) People by nature are fixers. We want people we care about to be whole, not broken. When great intentions go unchecked, it can lead to the distribution of unsolicited advice. Ad nauseam.

So how can you allow your friends or loved ones to say their peace and still keep your wits about you?

I'd say that whenever someone utters the phrase, "Have you tried …?" you will want to have a selection of prepared responses to help you out of these tight spots. People mean well; it's just that they don't realize they are the hundredth person who isn't a doctor or health professional to share their medical wisdom with you. Being a victim of people's insensitivities can frustrate you to the breaking point and we don't want that.

Even if you're interested in their advice, you can be proactive with any of these responses:

- I'd love to consider your ideas, but since I'm overwhelmed right now, would you mind sending it in an email to me instead?
- I'm completely confident with my treatment protocol, but thanks for thinking of me.
- I love my doctor and trust his advice implicitly, so we're covered. Thank you!
- If I'm ever in need of medical advice, I'll call you, but for now we've got it.
- I'm open to new ideas, but I'd love it if you share them with my medical advisor. Then they will share it with me when we have time and space to consider it.
- Right now, I don't have the margin to consider anything outside my current treatment protocol, but I appreciate your concern.

The medical side of your trial doesn't have to be a detriment to your health or the health of someone you love. If you're advocating for yourself or a loved one, trust your instincts. Keep good records. Take a friend or loved one with you to appointments. And above all, don't stick with a doctor or protocol you don't feel right about just to make someone else happy or save face. You are the primary beneficiary of the decisions you make, so take charge!

More Than One Way

I'll never forget the fear I felt before my first of four back surgeries. I didn't want to have surgery, but I had tried every other alternative to relieve my pain. Nothing was working—not acupuncture, physical therapy, chiropractic care, epidurals, rest, ice, heat, steroids, standing on my head for hours. (Okay, that last one was a joke, but I was the recipient of lots of medical advice.) Nothing worked, and it was looking like surgery was my only hope.

The doctors weren't hesitant to perform surgery. They said it would be a breeze, and I'd feel better in no time. But for some reason, I resisted because I felt like there was a continuum of healing, and surgery was on the very-worst-terrible-no-good side of that scale. I did after all have three children, ages five, three and one, and they were talking about cutting open my spine! I was so torn about this, I went to my pastor to talk about it. It was clear I was suffering and in lots of pain. When I told him my reservations about the surgery, he reminded me that

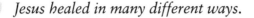

Jesus healed in many different ways.

Merely touching Jesus' robe healed the woman who was bleeding. The blind man was healed by mud placed over his eyes. The royal official's son was healed when Jesus wasn't even present. The demons were cast out of a man through prayer. Several blind men were healed by touch. And the list goes on.

To think we know the only way someone can be healed or have their prayers answered is simply false. Jesus is in charge of that. So, if you need medicine or, as in my case, surgery and it gives you your life back? Amen and another amen to that.

A Fork in the Road

I would be remiss if I didn't address an important topic that can polarize and isolate people: depression and anxiety. These illnesses are very real and affect more people than we realize. There are times when we can pray for relief and it will be taken from us, but there are other times we are suffering from a chemical imbalance that only medication can remedy. Taking medicine for depression or anxiety is not a sin.

Let me repeat that. It's not a sin to take medicine. People who suffer from clinical depression and anxiety can't always just "pray more" to be healed.

One woman who faced a deep and debilitating depression struggled with the decision to take medication because she thought it was a sign of weak faith. Her husband finally told her, "If you had any other disease, you'd be lining up to get the medicine the doctors prescribed. Mental illness is no different."

Once she began to take medicine, she said, "It gave me the coping skills I needed." She followed this protocol with regular counseling sessions and eventually determined the sudden onset was related to menopause. Over time, she weaned off the depression medications as she began to treat her hormone imbalance.

Another woman's husband had an affair and divorced her. Within months, she was diagnosed with breast cancer. After she found out about his infidelity, she said she struggled just to get out of bed for months. A friend called her each morning to ask if she was out of bed. If she wasn't out of bed, the friend would call back fifteen minutes later. She kept calling. Day after day. Finally, the friend told her, "I think you need some help. Medicine might be the right choice for you."

This woman said, "We need to be open about the possibility of medical intervention and get over the judgment of it. That medication was the catalyst I needed to pull me out of the pit. It helped get me back on track and begin to live my life again."

God gifts people to be doctors. Every single ability we have in modern medicine is a gift from God. He created the people's minds who create medicines. To say that one way of healing is better than another is pure arrogance. We aren't God. We don't get to decide how we are healed. For some it might be prayer, for some it might be medicine, for some it might be counseling.

And it very well could be a combination of all three.

Months after losing my best friend, I ended up in the emergency room with what was later diagnosed as an anxiety attack. That was the only time I have ever felt its physical effects—racing heart, numbness in my arms, and shortness of breath—but it was enough for me to understand what other people face. Counseling was the answer, and it helped me immensely.

My daughter has also experienced physical and emotional manifestations of anxiety. She asked us for help and then proceeded with Christian counseling. I'm so proud of how brave she's been and how she works to cope with it by implementing the practical tools given by her therapist. Seeing someone to help you, like a counselor, psychologist, or psychiatrist, is not a sin or sign of weakness.

The important thing is to admit you've got a problem and get the help you need for your depression or anxiety. Don't eliminate any options because you think they signal a lack of faith. There's nothing wrong with getting outside help from a trained professional, praying to God to free you from this pain, or taking medication.

God wants us to have an abundant life.

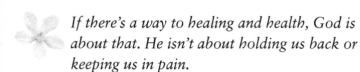

If there's a way to healing and health, God is about that. He isn't about holding us back or keeping us in pain.

CHAPTER 10
Traveling Buddies

Carry each other's burdens,
and in this way you will fulfill the law of Christ.
Galatians 6:2

Our family loves VeggieTales. If you're not familiar, VeggieTales is an animated children's series of movies, videos, and shows that teaches moral truths in a hilarious, meaningful way through animated vegetables as characters.

One favorite is *Jonah: A VeggieTales Movie*. In our estimation, Khalil, the caterpillar, steals the show. In one section of the movie, when Jonah gets swallowed by the fish, Khalil, who is his steady sidekick, wants to follow him. As he's being launched through the air like a cannonball after Jonah, he says, "I'm coming, traveling buddy!"

My husband, Craig, likes to put on his best Khalil voice and repeat that phrase at random times to me and our children. It makes all of us roll our eyes, even if we do secretly adore his quirky brand of humor. In fact, one time my husband texted a video of this scene to my daughter at college to let her know he was coming for a visit.

Yes. We are that family.

So, regardless of whether you've seen the movie (if not, you should) or if you have a silly streak like us, you've now been introduced to the concept of a traveling buddy!

A traveling buddy is simply someone who goes with you somewhere, sticks by your side and, I would argue, makes everything better.

And if you're in the middle of a hard place, like staring down cancer, coming through a divorce, raising a child with special needs, living with chronic illness, or walking through difficulty with aging parents, you *definitely* need some traveling buddies.

Four Buddies

Mark 2:1–10 tells the story of Jesus healing a paralytic man. It's an awesome account—also found in the Gospels of Luke and Matthew—of a man not only being forgiven of his sins but also being healed. But I'm all about verse 3, which says, "They came, bringing to him a paralytic carried by four men" (ESV). The paralytic was unable to get himself to Jesus. He couldn't walk. But he had some traveling buddies, and they brought him all the way to the feet of Jesus.

Even though the healing and forgiveness are a major part of the story, I want to focus on the four buddies. Can you imagine what those guys might have been thinking when they arrived at the place where Jesus was and there was "no more room in the hut"? There wasn't even standing room in the back. Nada. Nothing. No chance in Jerusalem they were getting inside those doors.

How frustrated they must have felt!

But these traveling buddies weren't taking no for an answer. Door's blocked? No room? We'll just dismantle the house to get our friend what he needs.

I've seen people do whatever it takes on behalf of a friend in need, just like these four traveling buddies. And I'm guessing you've seen it too, if not benefitted from it yourself.

Friends who drop everything to come over and watch your kids, so you can go to the hospital for the hundredth time. Neighbors who mow your grass or shovel your driveway when you're grieving and can't find your way outdoors. Coworkers who carry the extra load and take over the meeting or entire project, so you can miss work for your treatments. Family members who do your dirty laundry, clean your house, buy your groceries, and overlook your mess as you recover. Loved ones who sit quietly by your side, saying nothing, because there's nothing to be said.

Buddies who move heaven and earth to show you how much you're loved.

 It's a beautiful sight when people carry your mat and bring you before the throne of grace. But you have to let them.

My Mat

When my kids were young and I was a new Christian, I faced a difficult personal trial. Many of us know that, just because we turn our life over to Christ, it doesn't mean we won't have struggles or challenges. We have an enemy who is out to get us (Ephesians 6:12) and who will tell us lies about who we are if we let him.

As I mentioned earlier, I was an impressionable young girl who looked for love and approval wherever I could get it. Some of it was perfectly innocent and appropriate, like the relationships I had with teachers, both male and female, who built up my self-esteem and gave me a safe place to talk. But others were unhealthy and came in the form of dating relationships where I did whatever I needed to do in order to gain approval and affection.

So, I had a past. And the devil tried to use it against me. And for a time, he succeeded. You see, there was a man in my life who was a good friend to me. Whenever he said kind things to me, perfectly innocent on his part, I took them to heart, and they made me feel important and special. Pretty soon, I was having a one-sided emotional affair with this man.

Several things were terribly wrong with this picture. First, I was imagining all sorts of inappropriate scenarios and daydreaming about this man who was *not* my husband. Thankfully, he never had any idea of my feelings for him (and still doesn't to this day). Second, my husband, Craig, had no idea this was happening, and had done nothing wrong to warrant my emotional detachment. He has always been attentive, encouraging, and loving. I adore him.

I knew this behavior was wrong. I could even think it through to the end of any fantasy I had about being with this other man and see that it was unrealistic and not something I wanted. And I begged God to take away the thoughts I was having. I pleaded over and over again for forgiveness for what was going on in my mind. I didn't want to be with this man. I wanted the life I had with Craig and my three kids. But my impure thought-life had an unrelenting hold on me that I could not break free from on my own.

Finally, after months of internal torture and an ever-growing emotional chasm between me and my husband—even though he was unaware—I knew I needed help or I might do something I'd regret. It was in a moment of desperation and extreme humility that I turned to a few trusted Bible study friends who were walking life's road with me. We were fellow traveling buddies. I shared what I had been going through.

Initially, I was afraid to tell them because I thought they would think less of me. But I knew they were dependable, trustworthy people who loved the Lord. And honestly, I had no choice left. It was either tell another person and hope for the best or follow through with telling this man my feelings and risk the worst-case scenario playing out.

My friends received my confession with open ears and tender, grace-filled hearts. They didn't judge me; they merely pointed me toward truth and helped me find a way back to the marriage and man that I loved.

I was paralyzed by my own situation. I had tried everything and was finding no relief of my condition. And when I could not pick up my own mat and get myself to Jesus, my traveling buddies carried me to Him, and helped me find redemption and forgiveness. And they emboldened me to speak the truth to Craig, who offered more of the same. His wholehearted forgiveness was nothing short of a miracle in my eyes.

That's what grace is—undeserved merit or favor. I didn't deserve it, but my husband offered it freely. And in the end, he reminded me in no uncertain terms, "Sarah, you are no longer the girl who needs another man's approval to feel loved. That is not who you are. I know this is the enemy trying to take you out. God loves you unconditionally, and so do I. I forgive you."

I am a new creation. Loved by God. Saved by grace. And I made it through that dark time in my life because a few good traveling buddies dug a hole in the roof of my dirty, grungy sin and made a way for me to get to Jesus and receive forgiveness.

Truth Speakers

I call the traveling buddies who helped me out of my darkest pit my "truth speakers." Your truth speakers are people you trust to tell you what you need to hear, even when it's not easy or you don't want to hear it. They are people who meet you in the dark and fling open the closet doors to remind you that the boogie man isn't real, and God is bigger than your fears.

During her husband's four-year legal battle, Kassandra said one of the things that saved her was a woman who became her truth speaker. They weren't best or even close friends. But this woman's age and wisdom were beneficial to Kassandra when she needed it most.

One woman faced a miscarriage followed by a crisis in her marriage. When she found out she was pregnant again, she was devastated. As she wrestled with depression and anger, she admitted feeling discouraged and out of control, with nowhere to turn. She began to confide in a male coworker and over time their relationship escalated to an affair. Her situation was exacerbated by her struggle with depression, and she says she rationalized for far too long why she shouldn't confide in her husband or a good friend. Eventually, she summoned the courage to share her struggle with her husband and a truth-speaking friend.

She says, "I wished I'd reached out sooner. My advice is to reach out to friends before it gets too bad. Be proactive in your faith, praying, studying the Bible, and preparing yourself before the hard times come."

This couple did the hard work to get through their hard place and fought for their marriage. And now they're a redeemed, beautiful, and healthy family of three.

A Lonely Number

I'm an extrovert. So, it's no surprise that I like having people around. My life as the youngest of fourteen children may be responsible for this inexplicable need for camaraderie. Ever since I was little, I didn't like being alone or in quiet places. I spent years trying to get better at being alone, and I've learned to love it—even crave it! This proves we're never too old to learn something new.

What about you? If you're an introvert, don't tune me out! This is for you. You might have to learn how to be with other people, like I had to learn to be alone. Learn to lean on them, allow them in, especially when you're facing a challenging circumstance or time in your life.

Because even if you like solitude, when you are going through a hard time in your life, it's essential you don't try to go it alone. People who climb Mount Everest don't go alone, they bring a Sherpa, or guide, with them, who helps carry their load. Even introverts need truth speakers.

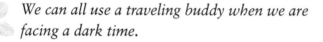 *We can all use a traveling buddy when we are facing a dark time.*

One of the most common pieces of feedback I received when I surveyed people asking what their biggest struggles were during their hard times, was loneliness.

How can we escape loneliness? We have to *ask* for what we need. (More on this later.) We have to reach out for help. Counselors, therapists, psychologists, psychiatrists, clergy, social workers, pastors, Bible study groups, mentors, friends. We might have to find a way to speak the words, "I'm lonely, sad, or scared today."

When I was grieving Kelley's death, my counselor was my saving grace. Her help and insight were invaluable. I couldn't have recovered or walked away from that experience healthy without her assistance. Sometimes, we don't know how badly we're suffering until we start to say some things out loud. That's the benefit of a counselor. None of us is above the wisdom and guidance from a trained professional. If nothing else, you've got someone who's paid to listen to you! And who wouldn't welcome that?

Do You Have Buddies?

If you don't have people who fall into Relationship Tier 1 or 2 in your life, find some. Or you may have to rely more heavily on a Tier 3 person if you live far away from close family or friends. You may also find that, during your crisis, people who were previously at Tier 3 in your life move their way into a higher category based on how they respond to your crisis. Some people are just wired for serving and coming alongside, so they naturally rise up in times of need. You might form a bond you didn't have before and they will now be someone you depend on. It's a gift when this happens.

Don't dismiss someone's offer just because they start out on a lower level tier in your life. But if you're not comfortable receiving their help based on the level of friendship you have, the relationship tiers can also give you the permission you need to "circle the wagons" and only allow Tier 1 or 2 people to be in the inner circle of your crisis.

When You've Been There

One of the best ways to take the focus off your own hard place is to be a traveling buddy for someone else. My friend Angie offers herself as a resource through Juvenile Diabetes Research Foundation for people to call when they receive a type 1 diabetes diagnosis. Over the years, she has given hope and encouragement to countless parents in her same situation.

The wisdom and advice of others has blessed Angie, too, in both her son's diagnosis and her own breast cancer journey. She attests, "I've learned way more from other moms of diabetics than I've ever learned from my son's specialists. I switched surgeons based on the advice of other women who'd had my same surgery. I bought clothes post-surgery based on the advice of others who knew what the challenges were. I've gotten some of my best perspectives by observing how other faith-filled friends approached their diagnoses."

When my brother was contemplating back surgery after decades of struggling with pain, I called him to offer insight and encouragement. I could share information that no one else could, because

I'd been there myself. Since I have the same genetic disease that causes weakened discs in our backs, I could paint a clear picture of the advantages and disadvantages of the surgery. And because my surgery was successful, and I have only moderate limitations, I could offer what he needed most—hope.

Psalm 40:9–10 (ESV) says, "I have told the glad news of deliverance in the great congregation. … I have spoken of your faithfulness and your salvation; I have not concealed your steadfast love." When we can proclaim what God has done in our lives and how we've overcome, that is an even greater gift to those we know facing similar pain.

Here are a few marching orders if you're inclined to come alongside another when you've been in their shoes.

Ask First

If you're considering sharing your experience to benefit someone else in a similar situation, ask if they'd like your advice before offering it. As someone who's been in a hard place yourself, you understand how vastly unhelpful unsolicited advice can be. So, if you're willing and able to offer insight, request permission before sharing.

Plant the Seed

If you aren't sure whether to share your own related story, make a casual reference to your own situation in conversation. If the person follows up by asking you a question about it, then proceed cautiously. If the first answer leads to another question, then it's likely they want to hear. If not, let it go.

Be content to plant a seed. If and when they are ready, they may seek you out for more information. Don't push if they seem to close down when you open the door. But do try again if you're feeling led. Be willing to open your mouth when God asks but also know when to keep it closed.

Tips for Sharing Your Similar Experience
- Show your vulnerability.
- Be brief.
- Don't minimize their situation.
- Don't one-up them by trying to make your situation sound more dire than theirs.
- Validate their feelings.
- Keep your heart motivations in check.
- Provide only information with direct correlation.
- Keep it first person. "Here's what happened to me." "This was my experience."
- Avoid trying to be the expert or telling them what they're doing is wrong.
- Don't process your grief with them or pour your emotions all over them.
- Use open-ended questions to determine if they are interested in your viewpoint.

Empty or Full?

When my children were young, I cherished any opportunity to get some "me" time away from the demands of being a full-time, stay-at-home mom. My husband often granted me a hall pass to get away for a few days alone or with friends during those challenging years of raising babies.

A favorite destination of mine is our lake place in Northern Minnesota. One wintry weekend, I headed north for a solo retreat in my hubby's four-door sedan. Despite the driveway at the vacation home being as steep as a ski hill, I left the four-wheel drive truck behind for him and the kids. That meant parking at the top of the driveway when I arrived because I'd never make it back up again in his front-wheel drive car.

Whenever I arrive at the cabin, I *hate* to leave—for any reason. I don't even like to drive the one mile to town for groceries. It's as if the moment I step across the threshold, I'm enveloped in a cocoon of relaxation. And unlike the butterfly, I'd prefer not to extricate myself.

That particular weekend was frigid cold. From snug in my bed under the covers, I checked my phone around 10 p.m. To my dismay, there was a weather alert on my phone. The temperature overnight was supposed to drop to −30 degrees. Yes. You read that right.

Thirty degrees below zero! Straight temperature, not including wind chill.

My next thought was even more disheartening. Even though I was low on gas that evening on my drive up, I didn't stop to refuel because I was anxious to get to the cabin.

It was ten o'clock at night, the car was at the top of the hill, it was already freeze-the-tear-ducts-in-your-eyes cold outside, and I was tucked in bed for the night. So, you can be sure I didn't want to leave my safe haven of comfort and peace.

However, any northern girl worth her salt knows the single most important truth about cold weather and vehicles: Never leave your car on empty overnight in sub-zero weather because your car won't start the next day! Not only was I raised with this mentality, but my engineer husband has reminded me of this fact more times than I can count.

I had a choice to make.

Stay in bed and take the risk. Or drag my sleepy self out of bed, hike up to the top of the hill, and drive to town to fill my tank with gas.

Which do you think I chose?

If you guessed that I stayed nestled in bed with sugar plums dancing in my head … you're wrong. Reason won the fight. That, and possibly fear of what my husband would say if I asked him to drive two hours to rescue me because of my laziness.

I climbed out of bed, bundled up, drove to town, and filled up the gas tank. Twenty minutes of my time, a few frozen eyelashes, and some cold toes, but potential crisis was averted.

Dear ones, hear this. Our lives will be filled with below-zero, out-of-gas-moments. If you're reading this book, chances are you're in the middle of one at this very moment.

But if we don't fill our proverbial tanks with gas before the freezing temperatures threaten to take us out, we will face the consequences.

Sometimes, we will fill up in the nick of time; other times it's a preemptive measure. Either way, a full tank is far better than running on fumes with no gas station in sight.

We need traveling buddies. We need truth speakers. We need people who will come alongside us and guide us when we've lost our way.

Sometimes, truth will come from the most unlikely source; other times it will come from a trusted friend. But right now, if you've got no one, I urge you to find someone. Fuel your tank of friendship. Fill your life with mat bearers who'd do anything to get you where you're going. Enlist truth speakers who won't break under the pressure or run the other way. Bring your painful story into the light with someone you trust, so they can help you find your way out of the dark.

No matter how painful that long walk uphill is in the dead of night, bundle up … and walk.

CHAPTER 11
Trail Markers

May these words of my mouth
and this meditation of my heart
be pleasing in your sight, Lord,
my Rock and my Redeemer.

Psalm 19:14

On most hiking trails, there are painted markers on rocks or signposts so that hikers know which way to go or to assure them that they're on the right path. When they haven't seen a marker in a while, it's wise to check if they're on the intended path.

If you've lost your way and it's getting to be dusk—like my family on our first hike in New Mexico—fear sets in. You might wonder, why didn't we tie ribbons to the trees like they do in the movies, so we could find our way home?

Because we are over-confident about our ability to always follow the path, that's why. That's a tough awareness, and one that's more common in the midst of hardship than you think.

In our case, we began with the best of intentions and then, all of a sudden, the sun was setting, we were low on water, and we'd lost the marked trail. And we happened to have three children along.

Panic set in, and we began to ask all sorts of questions of ourselves. How did we get here? Why were we not more careful about paying attention to the trail? Where did we go wrong?

In the middle of your personal desert, you may also feel like you've lost your way. Fear, questions, and doubt might line your path. Familiar markers may seem dim as darkness sets in.

That's why this chapter is filled with trail markers, so that you can mark the path with clear boundaries as you go, so you'll know how to stay on the path, even if it's a rocky one.

Because the known is so much better than the unknown—even if it's hard.

Take an Honest Inventory

Angie, who is a breast cancer survivor and has a son with type 1 diabetes, said these significant challenges caused her to take stock of those people she surrounded herself with and make some changes. Her husband was a catalyst for this honest assessment. He told her, "You only have so much energy. Why don't you conserve it for the people who fill you up right now, rather than the ones who take from you?"

After that, she started being more deliberate about who she would let help her, come over, stay for a visit, and so on. She says, "It really made a world of difference to take an honest inventory of people in my life who really made a positive impact."

Using the Tier System is another way to take inventory of who you allow into your struggle. If a Tier 3 person in your life continues to try to assert themselves where you don't want them, you don't have to let them in. You could simply say something like, "While I appreciate your offers and support, right now I've got limited margin and energy. I need to reserve it for my immediate family and closest friends."

One woman I interviewed stared down cancer and struggled with the negative mindset of a few family members. Because their attitude was detrimental to her health, she delayed telling them her diagnosis and avoided their calls because she couldn't handle their emotions. She remembers throwing her phone across the room because she was so frustrated by continuous negative attitudes. This additional stress was also affecting her health, so she had no choice but to confront her family with the truth.

She told her sister, "I need you to encourage me. Otherwise, you cannot come to visit me. Don't give me your anxiety. I can't be your support group."

Her conversation helped, for a time. Once she was in remission, her sister regressed so she had to lay claim to healthy boundaries again. She said to her, "Yes, I'm in remission and I'm feeling good, but I still need to heal. I can't handle your anxiety, stress, and worry."

One man whose wife had cancer told me that they changed her phone number because they couldn't handle the constant influx of questions, demands, and even concern.

You are not alone. Lots of people have been in your shoes and have made hard decisions and taken honest inventories.

Hang on to the people who lift you up and find a way to get distance from those who bring you down.

What you need in your time of trial is simply what you or your family need. It's not about other people right now. It's about your grief, your divorce, your child's needs, your parent's health, your diagnosis, your addiction, your recovery, your you-name-it.

Putting yourself first is not selfish; it's necessary. When you can take an honest inventory about who is helpful in your life and who is a detriment, you will be able to return faster to a healthy place.

Set Boundaries

I've learned the importance of following painted rocks or signposts when I'm hiking. The trouble comes when I leave the boundaries. Likewise, in the midst of our hard place, healthy boundaries protect us from the perils that await us off the trail.

After a biking accident, Joel was hospitalized for an extended period of time. He told me he had to ban his sister from visiting. Even the doctors and nurses agreed. Her toxic presence was a detriment to his healing. Sometimes, even if someone is a Tier 1 or 2, you will need to set healthy boundaries if they can't provide the support you need. If you're looking for more help in this area, I highly recommend reading Dr. Henry Cloud and Dr. John Townsend's updated edition of *Boundaries: When to Say Yes, How to Say No to Take Control of Your Life*

Unhealthy people aren't helpful in the middle of a crisis. Sometimes, we feel like we don't get to choose, but you can, and you should. Don't let an already dire situation be made worse because you didn't act on what you knew you needed.

When my friend Deborah was in her final days, I distinctly remember a Tier 3 person being adamant about a visit. By this point there was little extra margin for anyone but Tier 1 relationships. However, it was difficult to thwart her persistent efforts. I wished I had the courage on Deborah's behalf to tell her we were limiting visitors so Deborah wouldn't have expended precious energy she didn't have to spare.

This woman made it about her, when it should have been only about what Deborah wanted, needed, or could handle in those last days of her life.

Determine Your Non-Negotiables

If you were going on a trip to Europe, you'd plan for your journey before you left so you'd be able to accomplish all you set out to do and stay on task while you were there. But if you got dropped out of a plane in the middle of Europe with no preparation, you'd be unequipped for the location and your trip would be less than enjoyable.

Similarly, in a crisis, instead of constantly reacting to your circumstances, a bit of proactive planning will give you a head start.

You can stay focused and plan ahead by creating a list of your non-negotiables. This will ensure you stay on the right path and provide a better plan for the journey ahead. Think of this list as your painted rocks on the trail. Without them, you're prone to getting lost.

Patricia lost her mom and then helped care for her dad who died within a year. She was also a trustee for the family farm, which brought a whole new load of responsibility and emotion. When her family decided to sell the farm, she faced another form of grief. That period of time for her was filled with pain, sorrow, but also clarity. What was clear in the midst of it all was that her mom and dad were the central priority. Her top goals were to love her parents, provide care for their legacy, and honor her siblings. She knew with absolute certainty what her non-negotiables were.

Although that didn't make her weekly trips back and forth to the farm while managing a family and a full-time job any easier, she had set her priorities as a guideline for all her other actions. She says, "I had full margin for Mom and Dad, and zero for anything else. And it wasn't sad, it just was. I was 100 percent with them, and in full recovery mode at all other times."

Patricia had other priorities that allowed her to recover in between her trips to the farm, which included maintaining a strict exercise routine, cleaning up her eating, and focusing all her reading time on Scripture. Again, these non-negotiables helped her navigate a harrowing path, and maintain her ability to do what she felt called to do—love and honor her parents and their legacy.

The bottom line is you get to choose. You don't have to let other people's ideas of what you need dictate what you actually need.

If you don't determine what your absolutes are, they will be determined for you.

Think Before You Speak

In Alcoholics Anonymous, one of the phrases used to help people in recovery is "think through the drink." Processing the aftereffects of taking that first drink helps them to see that the end result is not nearly as glamorous as the quick fix they'd feel initially. Thinking through the consequences later deters desire in the moment.

Similarly, if you're angry, frustrated, and operating at limited capacity, you might be inclined to say something you'll later regret. The Bible tells us that the fruit of the Spirit is "love, joy, peace, patience, kindness, goodness, faithfulness, gentleness, self-control" (Galatians 5:22–23 ESV). I pray for these attributes of the Spirit, but I struggle most with self-control. Especially when it comes to control over my mouth! (I'm a work in progress.)

If you've been in a trial or an overly stressful time, you know when you're running on fumes it's easier to snap at people and say words you'll later regret. There are times we imagine how great it will feel to finally express what's on our mind to the person who is frustrating us. But if we think through the verbal explosion all the way to the aftermath it will leave behind, hope-fully we'll reconsider.

In the middle of a crisis is probably not the time to bring up old wounds either. If someone is aggravating you, there are healthy boundaries you can set with them without adding irreparable verbal damage to the list. You *can* choose not to chip in your two cents or bring up how they wronged you twenty years ago. Just sayin'.

If you really need to express something, wait, pray, and consider an appropriate time to discuss your grievances with the person. In the end, you'll feel better for not falling prey to the temptation to speak your mind in the heat of the moment. And you'll maintain necessary relationships with people you need to walk alongside you in your hard place.

Craft Your Response

Dealing with people's well wishes and pat one-liners can take its toll during hard times. Whether you're grieving and can't bear to hear one more person say, "I'm sorry for your loss," or you're tired of people asking how you're feeling, it's important to think in advance about how you might respond. This alleviates the tendency to express your frustration in an inappropriate or unhealthy way.

After the death of her husband, Karen B. was caught off guard by an acquaintance who stopped her in the grocery store and said, "Following you on Facebook, it's almost like you're doing too well!" Karen couldn't contain herself. She retorted, "I thought about taking a picture of myself curled up in the fetal position on the bathroom floor, but the lighting was wrong."

Friends, it's hard to be at the mercy of people's thoughtlessness! It's hard, day after day, to smile and nod and keep on keeping on in the midst of the deluge of both well-intentioned and not-so-tactful people who want to say *something* but don't know *what* to say. It's a challenge to put on a brave face and go to Target or the grocery store or church or the kids' sporting events and find a way to respond to all the desperate, pity-filled faces that want somehow to say the right thing.

Sometimes, we just lose it, like Karen did. (Honestly, I loved her reply, even if I don't advise it. I give her an A-plus for wit under pressure!)

Other times, we'll have a grace-filled response and try to make them feel better, even though it isn't our job. If you think about how you'll respond in advance, you might be able to avoid the "banana split" in the produce aisle.

Here are a few suggested responses for handling the monkeys out there:

- I'm conserving my energy, so I'd rather not go into it today. But I appreciate your interest and your support.

- If you want the comfortable answer, we're doing okay. If you want the real answer, it's hard.

- Thank you. We're sorry for our loss too.

- Thanks for your concern. It's hard to go over it all the time, so we post all the updates on the CaringBridge (or Facebook or whatever means you choose). That helps me conserve my energy.

- We're okay, considering the circumstances. At least I'm up and about today, which is more than I can say for most days. But I appreciate your concern.

- We're trusting God in the middle of it all. That doesn't always make it easier, but when we rest in God's truth it helps us press on.

Having your "talking points" ready prepares you for the Tier 2 and 3 people you'll encounter along the way who want to express their concern or sympathy. When you have zero margin left to talk about your trial one more time, a simple phrase, prepared in advance, will go a long way toward keeping you sane.

Another difficulty is knowing how to handle other people's public grief. Karen also struggled with this. She said people wanted to tell her stories about her husband or grieve his loss when she was with her kids. She found a way to handle this by saying, "I'd love to hear what you have to say about this. Could you write it down and send it to me in an email or by Facebook message?" She said that gave those people permission to express themselves in writing and not process their grief when she wasn't able to handle it.

As I wrote in *Alongside*, sometimes the grieving or ill person just wants "to go to Target and be normal," not have it always be about their problem. If you're feeling the weight of people's expressions of support and just want a bit of normal in the middle of your chaos, some prepared responses might be your solution.

Give Grace

We won't go through hard times without missteps. The first person you need to offer grace to is yourself. Merriam-Webster's online dictionary presents this definition of grace: *a temporary exemption; reprieve.* There is a time to give yourself a reprieve from the demands you normally place on yourself and others. And that time is when you're smack dab in the middle of the mess.

If you don't get the items on your to-do list done, so be it. If you have to put on a movie (or ten) for the kids in order to get through the day or the week, it's okay. If you fail in the keeping-your-mouth-closed department, apologize to the person you offended and move on. If you miss appointments, arrive late to activities, have a messy house for a while (even if it's a year), *let it go.*

 You don't have to traverse your hard place with perfection.

Some days it's a bonus if you just make it out of bed. Even when we're at full strength, we put pressure on ourselves to "perform." But when we set the same standards during a crisis, we are destined to fail! During chemotherapy, Linda made it her goal to do one thing every day. Even if that one thing was taking a bath, she considered it a success.

Grace. Upon grace. That is what you need to give yourself in the middle of the trial. Even if you don't think you deserve to rest, wait, stop, postpone, cancel, skip, or say no, I'm here to tell you that you *do*. And you can. If you'd tell your best friend, your sister or brother, or someone you care deeply for that it's okay for them to cut themselves some slack, then why isn't it all right for you to do the same?

Right. You've got no good answer for that. Neither do I. Placing unrealistic expectations on ourselves only adds to our stress, and it produces emotional, physical, and spiritual ramifications.

Likewise, we shouldn't be too hard on the people around us either. My friend David said the wrong thing to a friend who'd just lost a son. The friend was understandably upset with him and expressed his anger. Eventually, they hashed it out and moved on. But David *still* feels badly for choosing words that hurt instead of helped in that difficult moment. He said, "People who say the wrong things mean well. Cut them some slack; they're doing their best in a difficult situation too."

Giving grace to others can be challenging. But it's essential if we want people to stick with us and not abandon us in our trial because we have unrealistic expectations of them. Karen said, "After my husband died, I had to make myself approachable and be patient with people who didn't know how to express their support."

Remember, for our purposes, grace means an exemption or reprieve. It's not forever, but it never hurts to have a posture of grace with ourselves and others. Put grace on your plate each day and serve a side of grace to others. And top everything off with an extra dollop of grace!

Part 3:

Journey

The Lord makes firm the steps
of the one who delights in Him;
though he may stumble,
he will not fall,
for the Lord upholds him
with His hand.

Psalm 37:23–24

CHAPTER 12

Ask for Directions

*Ask and it will be given to you; seek and you will find;
knock and the door will be opened to you.*

Matthew 7:7

"It's about the journey, not the destination."

I'd be lying if I said that this expression didn't frustrate me beyond belief—like pulling-my-hair-out, don't-you-dare-say-that-to-me-one-more-time kind of frustration!

My husband is the biggest culprit. He sure means well, but what if, on the journey, he never reached where he was going? Would he be so quick to assuage me with those exasperating words *then*?

Sometimes, it's laundry I'm supposed to see as a beautiful, continual, never-ending journey. (I just need to finish it *all* sometimes.) Or on long car trips when I won't hardly let anyone stop for a potty break. My hubby urges me to pause and breathe and enjoy the journey. But seriously, we have a destination, and the sooner we're out of the car, the better! (Remember my trip to the cabin and how I didn't want to stop for gas? Yep, that's me.)

But as a big girl in a grown-up world, I've had to learn to live those words—embrace them even. It's a metaphor for so many situations, but also a fitting one for day-to-day life. Nitty-gritty life stuff, like doing laundry, going to work, driving the carpool, cleaning the house, raising the family, caring for elderly parents, watching sports, attending meetings, savoring vacations, putting kids to bed, sitting at someone's bedside … *and* walking through dark places.

But I concede, what's good for us isn't always easy.

This shift in thinking has contributed to my calmer demeanor on car trips and in life—learning to slow down, not trying to get to the end of everything in such a hurry and savoring the "through" and "during" instead of only the end.

If you're in the middle of your own dry and weary place, you might bristle at the "journey" word. You'd prefer to get the destination over and done with, not still be in a place where you have to go through this. I feel you! But together we can embrace our journey, because it's necessary.

Now that we have our packing list, team, gear, first aid, traveling buddies, and trail markers, we'll set out for the next phase of our journey. This section of the book will help you focus on the critical stops you'll need to make along the way.

First Stop

I also get frustrated by people who won't stop and ask for directions. My sweet, patient husband has no issue turning around if he misses an exit or makes a wrong turn. He's so chill. Meanwhile, I sit and stew about all the time we lost getting to our destination! (Like I said, I'm still a work in progress on the whole journey-not-destination mindset.)

Ironically, even though I'm anxious to get where we're going, I'm not hesitant to pull over and ask a simple question to get the help we need to get back on track.

Our journey through hardship is much the same. Even if we'd rather press on regardless of the possible negative outcomes, there will be times we'll need to ask for what we need.

Asking for help is difficult because it requires putting aside our pride, embarrassment, self-reliance, or shame in the name of getting our needs met.

And it won't always be as easy as a stop at the local gas station to find out which street to turn on to get where we're going.

The difficulty is that we want a solution to our problems, but we want a magic fix to appear without effort or communication. It would be great if everyone in our sphere of influence could antici-pate our needs and seamlessly supply exactly what we need with-out our intervention.

I wrote *Alongside,* for that exact reason—to equip people with practical, tangible ways to love others in difficult circumstances. However, we need to assume people can't read our minds (or haven't yet read my book!) and won't always know how to help us unless we ask them.

Catch 22

Here is the problem: We desperately need other people's help in the middle of our challenging circumstance, but we are afraid to ask. We feel like a burden so, rather than ask for help, we sit in misery.

We wait and wonder why no one understands how much we're hurting, how sad and lonely we are, how much pain we're in. We want visitors, but we feel vulnerable telling people that. We can't imagine what we'll do for dinner while we're laid up, but we wouldn't dream of asking someone to help us with a meal. We want friends, but we stay at home alone, never inviting people into our lives.

And then we hold everyone to this unrealistic standard—that they should know what we need or how we're feeling. Sadly, their first thought in the morning probably isn't, "Oh, she's facing this crisis; I bet she needs dinner." Or "Wow, I haven't seen him for a while. I wonder if he's depressed and lonely." Or "I wonder what she needs today. I'm sure she's so overwhelmed by all the time she spends caring for her aging mother."

It's a seemingly impossible jam we find ourselves in. But there is a solution.

To get over ourselves, open our mouths, and ask for help. Otherwise, those who care about us might never know we're in need.

Asking Brings Blessings

My husband and I were speaking at a marriage retreat and a woman approached me afterward to ask for advice. She confessed she was feeling lonely but was having trouble connecting at her church. With little kids and a part-time job, she felt isolated and had nowhere else to turn. She said the small groups were filled on the dates and times she could attend. She asked me for ideas on how she might connect with others to combat her isolation.

First of all, how brave of her to be vulnerable and ask me for help! Second, what an honor that she trusted me with this painful truth.

After we discussed her situation at length, I offered to introduce her to the pastor's wife, who was part of the team that hired us. Even though the online information said the class was full, the pastor's wife told her she'd be sure to get her and her husband a spot for the Sunday school class between services. Since finances were an issue, we were also able to secure her a scholarship, so they could attend. By the end of that conversation, this young mother had an awesome solution to her plight.

All because she asked for help.

If she hadn't reached out to me (or someone else), she'd likely still be at home alone suffering and wondering how to improve her situation. Blessings can come from the most unexpected of places. Even the humble place of asking for what you need.

Courage to Ask

It seems if we have an "average" hardship like surgery, we can fall between the cracks when it comes to getting the help we need. We incorrectly classify our struggle as unworthy of help compared to a more grave hardship like cancer or death of a loved one.

Everyone's struggle is worth another's love and concern. There isn't a hierarchy of needs. We are the chief culprit in assuming our situation doesn't measure up.

A good friend of mine faced a six-week recovery following knee surgery. As she was on crutches, she couldn't work or take care of her family. Within the first weeks after her surgery, a few precious people brought meals and walked her dog, but otherwise she wasn't really on anyone's radar. By week three of her recovery, she couldn't keep up with her family's needs, yet she was afraid to ask for help.

While we chatted on the phone one day, she acknowledged her plight. Feeding her family was a top priority, as her husband and two children were busy with work and school, and she couldn't stand on crutches to shop or cook.

Her church has a meal ministry, but she was hesitant to ask them to help her. Finally, I convinced her she was worthy of the help of her church family, and she agreed to reach out and ask for the resources she needed to get through the next three weeks of recovery.

She wrote an email to the person in charge of the meal ministry and received this loving response: "We will absolutely, positively be able to help. A wise woman once told me to never refuse help. We will get this set up and bring a cooler and some food. We all have seasons in our life that connect us to our faith family more and less. As you have been serving Christ, let us serve you now. Nothing separates us from Christ's love. Romans 8:38–39."

When she got the reply, she texted me and said, "I could cry. Actually, I am crying. Thanks for the push." In my friend's situation, a simple email was all it took to get the help she sorely needed. Having the courage to ask was the hardest part.

If people in your life don't reach out and offer to help you in your distress, does it mean they don't care? No. It just means they aren't constantly thinking of other people's needs. And that's okay.

There are times we have to take matters into our own hands and get what we need or simply go without. And going without isn't a great option.

Make Your Requests Specific

In my friend's case, asking specifically for what she needed made it so much easier for the church to help. You can benefit from this same strategy. When you're reaching out for help, make your request as specific as possible.

Following her husband's death, Karen found an ingenious way to ask specifically for what she needed. She kept a running list of tasks or chores she needed done. When people asked her what they could do, she offered them the list. Doing this allows you the option of saying, "If you'd like to help, I have a list of what we need. If there's something on the list that suits you, we'd be grateful for the help."

This also takes the pressure off you to come up with assignments when people ask what they can do, while still giving them an out if the items on your list aren't something they feel they can do. It also provides ways Tier 1 and 2 people, who might be spending more time with you, to serve you without constantly asking what you need.

When you ask for help, be sure you always give people the option of saying no. Try not to pressure them, but at the same time, don't be apologetic. When you kindly and clearly ask for what you need in a humble way, everyone wins. You get the help you desperately need, and your loved ones are blessed by helping you!

Finally, be conscious to spread the blessing. In other words, don't take advantage of a few people just because it's easier to ask them. You will burn them out. Try to ask different people and be open to utilizing those who've offered but haven't helped before. Another great way to diversify your help is to inquire about existing programs or services that might offer what you need. (Think of my friend and the meal ministry, or the lists in chapter 8.) If you are still having trouble asking, enlist a close friend, family member, or your COO to make requests for help on your behalf.

Turn "Let Me Know" into Tangible Help

As you know by now, well-meaning people might not know what you need. It's up to you (or someone close to you) to take their generic "let me know if I can help" and turn it into a tangible "here's what you can do." Any of the following tasks are great ways to involve people who are Tier 2 or 3 relationships.

- ✓ Errands
- ✓ Grocery shopping
- ✓ Yard work/gardening
- ✓ House cleaning
- ✓ Pet care
- ✓ House care/sitting
- ✓ Rides to appointments (consistently is best)

- ✓ Meals
- ✓ Fundraising
- ✓ Driving children
- ✓ Childcare
- ✓ Daily activities/chores
- ✓ Visits
- ✓ Meal clean-up
- ✓ Laundry
- ✓ Breakfast or lunch, especially if you are home alone recovering
- ✓ Use of their car or house for your visiting family/friends

If you're unsure what to say when a Tier 2 or 3 relationship says, "Let me know what I can do," here are a few suggestions:

- I've learned that I can't navigate this road alone. I'd be grateful for the help. I have a few things you can choose from that we need if you'd like.

- I'd love help with _____, if that's something you're comfortable with or have time to do. If not, tell me what you were thinking and maybe we can find a fit.

- What kind of time do you have: ten minutes, two hours, or a half a day?

- Is there something specific you're interested in helping with?

- I appreciate the offer, but right now we are all set. But check with my COO in about a week or two and maybe then they will be able to tell you something we need.

- We are in need of meals if you'd like to bring a meal sometime.

- Check back in [insert time frame here], and I'll see if something you can do has cropped up.

When They've Been There

When we go hiking on a new trail, I'm constantly asking people who are coming from the other way about what lies ahead. My kids hate when I do this, but my motto is "There's no one better to ask than someone who's already been there."

This couldn't be more true when we are facing a trial of any kind. People who have already journeyed your path can be an invaluable resource for you.

When Tiffany first learned her daughter's diagnosis, she reached out to anyone she could find to ask them what to expect and to get her questions answered. When I was debating over spinal fusion surgery, I called three different people who'd had the same surgery and asked all my questions. When my neighbor Deborah was given a terminal diagnosis and was deciding about hospice care, she asked me about my experience with my friend Kelley, so she could make a wise decision about how to proceed.

When my daughter first experienced an anxiety attack and I didn't know how to help her, I sought wise counsel from a family member who had faced the same issues. Her insight helped me find solid ground in unfamiliar terrain. She also validated my daughter's condition while at the same time assuring me that neither of us had done anything "wrong." She helped me understand that, while my daughter's concerns didn't seem rational to me, they were very real to her. This helped alleviate my frustration when she had an anxiety episode and also helped me to seek out ways to help alleviate these symptoms instead of getting angry because they didn't make sense.

On her recommendation, my daughter sought the counselor who has helped her immensely over the years.

We're ignorant if we think we can do it all alone or that no one has advice we can benefit from. If someone you know, or a person you can trust based on the recommendation of a good friend, has been in your shoes, you'd be wise to seek them out as a resource to help you traverse your new terrain.

Ask for Prayer

When I was embroiled in my emotional affair, it's no surprise I also experienced increased back pain. One of the things I did to counteract my fear of ending up back on the surgical table was to reach out and ask for prayer. Although I reserved the intimate details for my trusted traveling buddies, I did ask a larger group of people to come together for a prayer meeting at church. I told them I was working through an issue that was affecting my health, and I wanted them to join me in praying for physical healing and release from fear.

I experienced immense relief after that prayer meeting. It was one more layer of confession, in a way, but it also allowed me to take advantage of the collective power of prayer. If I hadn't told people I had a need, they wouldn't have known to pray. I had to ask for what I needed.

It can be humbling to ask for prayer, but we can also get sidetracked by the notion that we are unworthy of prayer. Yes, there will always be someone who is worse off than you, but God isn't in the business of categorizing our prayers! He is Sovereign and "able to do immeasurably more than all we can ask or imagine" (Ephesians 3:20). So why do we think we should limit our prayers to only the most desperate of circumstances? If it's pride that's standing in your way of asking for prayer, then let me remind you the Bible says pride can lead to our demise (Proverbs 16:18).

Most people want to help, just like you'd want to help them if the roles were reversed. But you can't assume they should know how you feel or what you're lacking at any given moment. And it's a gift to them when you allow them to lighten your burden, even the smallest bit.

But it requires you to ask.

And then to receive.

CHAPTER 13

Quench Your Thirst

Wait for the Lord,
be strong and take heart.

Psalm 27:14

Plants are created to be nourished by something outside themselves. Some wouldn't even exist unless someone dug up the soil, placed them there, and watered them faithfully. External forces of water, sun, soil, and animals affect them and are pivotal in their survival. They are innocent bystanders in the whole growth and life process.

Human beings require external resources too. Water, food, clothing, shelter, human contact, and even vitamin D sustain life. Without them, eventually we'd wither away and die.

Therefore, it stands to reason that, in the midst of personal valleys of hardship, we'll need the external boost of something besides ourselves. And all we have to do to get this benefit is be open to receiving it.

There are plenty of us who think we can handle everything on our own. Or even who think doing so is a symbol of prowess, independence, or strength. A Superwoman letter "S" on the front of our work uniform, sweatshirt, business suit, or bathrobe (hey, I do my best work in my pajamas) would be appropriate—and welcomed—thank you very much.

Some of us embody more two-year-old stubbornness than others, but we each carry a bit of this "I-do-it-myself" mentality. Even if we falsely believe it's easier to do things ourselves, burnout will become our companion before long. And we will pay the price emotionally, physically, and even spiritually.

As we discussed in the last chapter, it's difficult to ask for what you need. But, it's also a challenge to receive help when people offer it. But like plants, receiving help from others is the living water that helps us survive. And we'd do well to learn how to accept it—sooner rather than later.

I Sent a Boat

There's a popular tale circulating the internet that describes a man who was trapped on top of his house during a flood. As the floodwaters rose, he prayed for God to save him. As he sat there praying, first a canoe, then a police boat, and finally a helicopter each stopped and offered him a ride to safety. To each offer of rescue, he politely declined saying, "No thanks. I prayed to God and He's going to save me."

Finally, the waters overtook his home and the man drowned. When he ended up in heaven at the pearly gates, the man inquired of God, "I prayed to you for help. Why didn't you save me?" The Lord replied, "I heard your prayers. I sent a canoe, a boat, and a helicopter. But you never got in."

Lest you think this is some parable that doesn't apply to you, let me share my friend Robin's story.

When she was at one of her lowest points in her cancer journey, Robin remembers standing in her kitchen one day trying to figure out how to cook dinner for her family. She had zero energy and everyone who could cook was at work. She prayed, "Lord help me. I don't know how I'm going to care for my family." The same day she prayed to God for help, her pastor called and offered meals. Her immediate response? "No thanks, we're okay."

Her friend and pastor insisted. Robin said, "Thankfully, she didn't take no for an answer. She told me they had meals all assigned and would be providing them every day for the next month!" She was overcome with gratitude, knowing God answered her prayers, even if she had difficulty accepting how.

Sometimes, we neglect to see God's provision when it's right in front of us because we don't like the source or the means He uses to deliver it. But when God supplies our every need, we must acknowledge that even if we don't like the *how*, we can't argue with the *what*.

Roadblocks

In writing this book, I surveyed hundreds of people. I asked what their greatest struggle was in the middle of their hard place. Many people indicated that they either didn't want to ask for help or felt like a burden to others. A huge percentage of people also said they were isolated, overwhelmed, depressed, hopeless, and afraid.

So, if we're drowning in our circumstances, why don't we accept help? Because we feel too guilty to receive help, too ashamed we have a need, or too prideful to listen to the advice of people who care about our welfare. These roadblocks stand in the way of getting what we need.

Friend, let me tell you something important.

 Being in need is not a sign of weakness; it's a sign that we're human.

We must reevaluate our priorities and get out of our own way.

During her battle with breast cancer, Carrie struggled with receiving. "It's so hard to be the receiver when you've been raised to be a giver. I cried when I had to receive and accept things graciously. People thought I was crying because I was grateful, but I was really crying because it was so uncomfortable! Over time it led me to a place where I could receive better and ask for what I needed."

When Linda, a cancer survivor, was undergoing chemotherapy, she accepted help. But since other people she knew were fairly independent during radiation treatments, she didn't think she'd need help with rides. She said, "What I didn't realize is those people hadn't gone through chemotherapy before radiation. I was still weak from the chemo and couldn't drive myself to the radiation center. My husband set up rides with the local American Cancer Society office. It was uncomfortable accepting help from strangers, but in the end, I did appreciate it."

Do we want to get through our personal desert? Or do we want to get through it alone, without the help of others? Either way, we get through; one way is just easier than the other.

We can also falsely assume everyone sees us as our circumstance when, in fact, most people aren't thinking of us at all! Most people are living their life, doing business as usual, and getting by day-to-day—just as you would be if you weren't in your own personal desert.

Don't assume everyone "knows" your business. Don't believe the lie that accepting help makes you weak. Don't let the roadblocks of shame, embarrassment, guilt, self-reliance, pride, or isolation stand in your way of receiving the blessing of others. Those feelings overtake common sense and will only compound your problems.

Instead, as you walk through this dry, parched land, reach out and accept that cup of cold water from a friend and allow them to quench your thirst.

Robbery

As I faced multiple back surgeries, it was difficult for me to surrender and receive help. Regardless of how unrealistic the notion was, I wanted to pretend I had a letter "S" on my PJs as I lay in my bed. Early on, my wise husband pulled me out of my self-sufficient daze. He said, "I know you'd much rather give help than receive it. I also know how much joy you get from helping people. But if you don't let people serve you, then you're robbing them of that same joy of helping you."

I couldn't argue with his logic. I knew from my own experience how I cherished coming alongside and serving others in their hard places. But what if they didn't allow me to help? That would be a sad thing for me. When I thought about it in those terms, I relented. From then on, I never turned away help when I needed it.

If you are wondering if you should accept someone's offer of help, before you decline it, first ask yourself two questions: 1) Do I need what this person is offering? 2) Would I be taking away the gift of allowing someone to serve me if I decline their offer?

No Obligation

Many people want to help you and will continually offer. If you don't need anything, or if you're not comfortable receiving help from someone for any reason, you don't have to say yes. Maybe they are a Tier 3 or 4 relationship, the task isn't suited to them, or you feel pressured to come up with things for people to do.

Astrid said, "It was stressful when people asked, 'What can I do to help?' I sometimes felt I had to give people tasks to help them feel useful."

If you're feeling burdened to create tasks or you truly don't need help, here are some ways to respond to well-meaning friends and family:

- I appreciate your offer, but right now we're covered. I'll add your name to the list if we come across something we need.

- Check back with me in a week or two. Right now, I don't have anything specific I can think of.

- If you come up with something you're able and willing to do, feel free to email or text me your idea and we'll get back to you if it works.

- Please don't be offended, but right now it's more work for us to come up with things for people to do, and we're just trying to stay afloat.

One final caution: Be sure you aren't saying no for the wrong reasons. If you need help, accept it, no matter how hard it is.

The Biblical Take

You might wonder if there is any biblical basis for this notion of allowing others to care for you in your trial. The answer is yes. The Bible says we are to love our neighbor as ourselves (Matthew 22:39), do our part to build up the body of Christ (Ephesians 4:16), carry each other's burdens (Galatians 6:2), and use our gifts to serve others (1 Peter 4:10), to name just a few. So, if you don't receive the help of others, you are preventing God's people from operating in their full capacity of faith and service.

Jesus said, "It is more blessed to give than to receive" (Acts 20:35). To whom does one give if there is no one to receive? Accepting help builds others up and enables them to do God's will. That is a gift only someone in need can offer. Consider it your act of obedience.

By receiving the gift of someone's heartfelt expression of care and concern, you're building the kingdom of God.

Opportunity Knocks

When we receive from others, we have a chance to grow. It's easy to be the person who gives; it's harder to be the person who accepts. We can grow in our capacity to be both humble and grateful when we allow others to help us. Trust me, I've been on the receiving end of more help than ten people put together! Although it's not easy, it's helped me develop a new appreciation for other people when I'm on the giving end. I know firsthand what their reservations are in receiving my offers of help, and I can counteract them because I have been in their shoes.

Another way you can grow is in the friendships and depth of relationships you will gain when you allow someone to come alongside you in your hardship. My neighbor Deborah lost her husband and, just two years later, was diagnosed with breast cancer. At the time of her husband's death, we were Tier 3 acquaintances. But after her husband's death, she accepted my offers of help and we slowly became Tier 2 friends.

When her cancer became terminal, we spent many hours together planning her funeral and attending to her affairs. Our friendship was based on mutual affection, common interests, and a foundation of trust because we'd shared the worst and best times.

I was privileged to be present for the last moments of her life and to deliver a eulogy at her funeral. If she'd never allowed me to help her in the first struggle, I wouldn't have been there for her final one. And I wouldn't have gained a treasured friend.

There's so much more to receiving help than just allowing someone to do for you what you can't do for yourself. There's an opportunity to develop character traits of humility, gratitude, and even being a good friend.

And there's always the chance that, when you allow someone to be the living water that quenches your parched soul, you might grow a little in the process.

CHAPTER 14
Gather Your Daily Bread

Trust God from the bottom of your heart;
don't try to figure out everything on your own.
Listen for God's voice in everything you do,
everywhere you go;
He's the one who will keep you on track.

Proverbs 3:5–6 MSG

The book of Exodus tells about the Israelites escaping from slavery in Egypt. After they safely crossed the Red Sea on dry ground, the walls of water receded into a watery grave for their pursuing enemies, the Egyptian army. Safely ensconced in the wilderness on the other side, they celebrated their newfound freedom. But before long, the Israelites began to grumble to their new boss, Moses.

First, they groaned about being thirsty. So, God provided water.

Next, they complained of hunger. So, Moses pleaded with God on their behalf. God agreed and provided manna for the Israelites. But there were a few conditions.

Moses said to the people, "It is the bread the Lord has given you to eat. This is what the Lord has commanded: 'Everyone is to gather as much as they need'" (Exodus 16:16).

God delivered bread (manna) six mornings a week. It was a literal picnic from heaven each day. You might be familiar with the story, but two important elements deserve our attention. First, the bread was given each morning. Second, they were only to collect enough manna to last for one day, except for the sixth day, when they were allowed to collect for two days to account for the Sabbath rest day.

Because they were to collect the food they needed only for the day, it's no accident that we now use the phrase "daily bread." The origination of the term comes from this forty-year time period when God gave the Israelites manna every day. Their daily bread.

And even though they were not supposed to store up more manna than they could eat in one day, they didn't listen. "Some of them paid no attention to Moses; they kept part of it until morning, but it was full of maggots and began to smell. So Moses was angry with them" (Exodus 16:20).

Why would God ruin perfectly good food just because those poor, hungry Israelites wanted to stash it under their pillows for a midnight snack? Because he wanted them to trust Him to provide what they needed each day.

Jesus reminds us of this concept in the Lord's Prayer. He tells us we're to ask God to "give us this day our daily bread" (Matthew 6:11 ESV). Not only that, Jesus makes this powerful declaration: "I am the bread of life. Whoever comes to me will never go hungry" (John 6:35).

So, what does all that biblical history mean for us today?

As we wander through our own deserts, God wants us to trust Him to deliver exactly what we need each day, both literally and figuratively. God was perfect in His provision then. And He's perfect in His provision today.

Our daily bread might come in many forms. Encouragement from a friend. A good test result. A positive outcome. A gift on the doorstep. A check in the amount you needed to pay your rent. A visit. A needed Bible verse. Answered prayer. A perfect song. An expedited appointment. A knowledgeable doctor. A task completed without asking.

We need to recognize that sometimes "daily bread" is all we'll get! Only what we need today. The problem arises when we look, wonder, worry, and stress about the future.

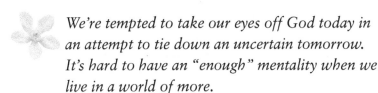

We're tempted to take our eyes off God today in an attempt to tie down an uncertain tomorrow. It's hard to have an "enough" mentality when we live in a world of more.

But we can trust God to provide our "manna" one day at a time. Sometimes, it will even be one second at a time. When our feelings aren't congruent with our faith, we can all use a little help.

Sources of Daily Bread

My daughter and I suffer the same plight. When we're hungry, no one can tell us we're hungry and that we need to eat. It's a terrible conundrum because, if we'd just eat something, everything would be better. But well-meaning people who make endless suggestions of meal or food options only fuel the flame. They'd better watch their head, or we'll bite it off! When we're finally fed, our "hangry" (hunger + angry = hangry) subsides, and we can listen to reason. It's just too bad that we have to let it escalate to that point before we do.

The options for sustenance provided in this chapter are like a menu from which you can choose your own "daily bread." The ideas are meant to be provision, not cause for duress. If one choice doesn't suit you, you aren't doing anything wrong. We all have our own taste, a complex palate designed by God. Implement what works for you.

But don't wait until you're so hungry that you won't listen to anyone! Be proactive and stay on top of that "hunger" to avoid the dreadful aftermath of waiting too long to collect your daily bread.

1. Try Something Different

In the face of her chronic health struggles, Susie admits she sometimes wrestles with "my feelings not resembling my faith." In other words, she has a strong belief in God, but there are times she doesn't love her circumstance. She offers this advice,

"When you're stuck, try something different, instead of trying harder."

Instead of working harder to fix the unfixable, don't be afraid to branch out and seek other means of hearing truth and hope.

For Susie, her quiet time has been a lifelong discipline. But there was a season when she felt like discipline had become a god and she needed to free herself from the duty of doing the same thing over and over. In order to feel God's presence afresh, she replaced quiet time with listening to music and it helped her get out of the rut.

The following are some different ways to seek spiritual solace and truth:

- Listen to Christian praise and/or worship music.
- Color in an adult coloring book with a biblical focus (try the Psalms).
- Read a devotional book each day.
- Start a new Bible reading plan on www.biblegateway. com or www.youversion.com.
- Attend a Bible study.
- Read through the Psalms.
- Memorize a focus Bible verse.

- Paint or draw a favorite quotation or Bible verse for your car, house, or hospital room.
- Find a worship concert in your area to attend.
- Sing your favorite hymn or song.
- Play an instrument you love.
- Listen to an audio passage of the Bible while you're doing other things.
- Recite Scripture out loud.

2. Seek Others

Another form of daily bread comes in the form of trusted traveling buddies. In your hard place, one way you can survive is to vent to someone who understands your plight or, at least, is willing to listen to your grumblings. If you need to dump your junk, pour it out in the safe space of a friend or loved one. If you carry it, it will weigh you down and make it difficult to keep going.

Frustrated? Call someone who's been in your shoes for empathy or advice. Doubtful? Reach out to a friend who is there to speak truth, without judgment. Feeling blue? Make time to spend with a positive person in your life who is a great listener. Coping with a chronic illness? Consider a coffee date with someone who shares the same reality. Afraid? Reach out to your pastor to get needed perspective. Anxious? Schedule an appointment with a Christian counselor. Never hurts to pay someone to listen to you, I always say!

We all need outside voices from time to time to combat the lies the enemy speaks or the untruths we tell ourselves. Remember, your job is to ask for the help you need.

3. Marinate in the Truth

God's promises are a bedrock to us in times of trouble. The wealth of affirmations available to us in His Word can become a form of daily bread. We marinate food for hours so the flavors seep in slowly, which improves the taste when we cook it. Similarly, marinating our minds with truth brings out the flavor of God when we come under fire. Biblical promises are seared into us, and truth can't be extricated from who we've become.

If you want to steep your mind in truth, start with these promises:

- The joy of the Lord is my strength. (Nehemiah 8:10)
- No weapons formed against me shall prosper. (Isaiah 54:17)
- God alone is my portion and my cup. (Psalm 16:5)
- God makes my lot secure. (Psalm 16:5)
- God began a good work in me and will bring it to completion. (Philippians 1:6)
- God fills me with joy in His presence. (Psalm 16:11)
- God will never leave or forsake me. (Deuteronomy 31:6)
- God is my refuge, strength and ever-present help. (Psalm 46:1)
- God has given me a spirit of power and love. (2 Timothy 1:7)
- God's peace will guard my heart and mind. (Philippians 4:7)
- Nothing will separate me from Christ's love. (Romans 8:38–39)

Another way to immerse yourself in truth is through Christian music. Few sources bring me more comfort and focused time on God than listening to biblical messages found in music. What I love is that it offers me the option to multitask. I play Christian music in my car, in my bathroom as I get ready in the morning, on my walks, and in my office. I'm all for the full-immersion approach!

The Bible is our first source, of course, but many talented musicians have found a way to bring those words to life in the form of music to minister to our souls. Don't underestimate the value of filling your mind with lyrics and song snippets that will come back to you when you need them most. And if your radio's default is your local Christian station, there will be many times when the perfect song will come on when you finally have a minute to yourself to feel your emotions.

I've also found that personalizing Scripture with your own name in it is a valuable way to focus your mind on truth. Check out my website at www.sarahbeckman.org/printable-scripture-cards to get your own download of these customized printable verses to encourage you or a friend. Another great option for Scripture inspiration can be found at www.marydeandraws.com/p/printables.html where you can print beautiful Bible verse coloring sheets.

4. Change Your Scenery

The beginning of Psalm 23 is one of the most familiar passages of Scripture: "The Lord is my shepherd; I shall not want. He makes me lie down in green pastures. He leads me beside still waters. He restores my soul" (Psalm 23:1–3 ESV).

We often associate these words with funerals, but I think these words are a gentle way of encouraging us to change our scenery. God is leading us to rest, possibly even outdoors in the green grass, if you can manage it, maybe in a park with trees and flowers. Even if you're not lying down, you're being still in His creation. It's no coincidence the words say that He makes us lie down, because for most of us the last thing we want is to slow down and consider our present circumstance. Some of us need a firmer hand when it comes to rest! But when you think of those words, they ought to evoke a sense of peace.

Rest isn't something we should resent; it's something we should seek.

Think of this phrase and imagine God's hand guiding you to the place where He's waiting to meet you.

My personal favorite part of this passage is, "He leads me beside still waters." Any excuse to take a bath, I'm in! Try a scented Epsom salt bath, complete with candles and soft music. If a bath or hot tub isn't your thing, walk around a lake or pond, or sit by any moving water, like a stream, and listen to the soothing sound of the water. Or purchase a small water fountain for your home, office, or hospital room.

Both green pastures and still water are designed to do one thing—restore your soul.

If you can't manage the time for any of the above options, consider a walk, hike, outing to the hospital cafeteria or gift shop, or a leisurely stroll to the mailbox. Maybe your change of scenery is a different room in your house as you recuperate, or relocation to a chair in the sunshine or outdoors. Even a shower or a visit to the laundry room can help relax your mind and clear your head. No matter the method, changing your environment brings welcome refreshment for the spirit.

5. Dwell in Today

As we learned, the Israelites weren't the best at focusing on today. But we can do better. We have the benefit of hindsight! One woman who responded to my survey said this: "We have a tendency to give up when we stew on the past or future. The past feels so organized and complete because it's already happened. It makes the current time look worse by comparison. The future can unfortunately wreak havoc with our fears when we are projecting from difficult circumstances. It's best to focus on the 'now' and accept the situation as is so you can face it head on."

She referred to two Scriptures that helped her maintain this one-day-at-a-time mindset: Matthew 6:34, "Do not worry about tomorrow, for tomorrow will worry about itself. Each day has enough trouble of its own;" and Isaiah 43:18, "Forget the former things; do not dwell on the past."

I love how those Scriptures helped steady her focus! In a world of pain and hurt, we need a daily-bread mentality. When we focus on what God can provide today, we won't dwell on the past or worry about the future.

CHAPTER 15

Seek the Source

Rejoice in hope, be patient in tribulation,
be constant in prayer.

Romans 12:12 ESV

Horatio Spafford, a Chicago businessman in the nineteenth century, had a wife, Anna, and five children. In 1871, they lost their only son to an illness and much of their business to the Great Fire. In 1873, Anna and their four girls traveled by sea on a French ocean liner to Europe. Mr. Spafford could not travel with them because he needed to attend to some business but planned to take another ship and meet them a few days later.

Four days into the journey, the ship, the Ville du Havre, collided with another vessel and began to sink. Anna Spafford and her four daughters knelt on the ship's deck praying for God to spare their lives, should it be His will, or to help them endure their fate. The ship sunk within twelve minutes. Out of the ship's 313 passengers, 226 died that day, including the four Spafford daughters.

Mrs. Spafford was found floating on a piece of wreckage and pulled from the sea by a sailor in a rowboat. Anna was later brought ashore in Wales, where she sent a telegram to her husband that began, "Saved alone, what shall I do?"

Mr. Spafford immediately booked passage to meet his grieving wife. Four days into the ship's journey across the Atlantic, the ship's captain notified Spafford that the ship was crossing the area where the Ville du Havre had sunk. According to one of Spafford's daughters born after this tragedy, her father penned the lyrics to the famous hymn, "It is Well with My Soul," while he was on this journey.

This verse is particularly poignant:

When peace, like a river, attendeth my way,
When sorrows like sea billows roll;
Whatever my lot, Thou hast taught me to say
It is well, it is well, with my soul.

This song still resonates with many church goers today. Likely because it was written from a place of utter despair. I appreciate these words so much because of the sentiment that no matter what circumstance we face we can learn to say, and believe, it is well with our soul. That, to me, is true faith. But these words are also a form of prayer for the grieving man who wrote it, and they can be for us, too.

Hymns are a powerful way of praying, whether they are sung or read in silence. The book of Psalms is also referred to as "songs of praise," and many of them were written as songs to be sung or chanted. Psalms were also a form of prayer and remain so today.

Prayer connects us with the source of comfort, truth, victory, identity, praise, holiness, and goodness. It's a critical part of surviving the storms of life. There are many ways to pray. And there's no right or wrong way, or good or bad time, to pray. What follows is ideas and forms of prayer for you to explore if you're not praying this way already.

May you find solace as you seek the source of power through prayer.

Pray Truth

When the world around you seems to be falling apart, try praying Scriptures that proclaim what God says about you, not what the world says about you. You can insert your name in the verse or phrase to personalize a truth.

Here's a list to get you started:

- I am chosen by God. (Colossians 3:12)
- I am holy and dearly loved. (Colossians 3:12)
- I am forgiven. (Colossians 3:13)
- I am blessed. (Ephesians 1:3)
- I am a conqueror. (Romans 8:37)
- I can approach God with confidence. (Hebrews 4:16)
- I can find mercy and grace in my time of need. (Hebrews 4:16)
- I am filled with God's strength. (Philippians 4:13)
- I am loved with an everlasting love. (Jeremiah 31:3)
- I am God's handiwork. (Ephesians 2:10)
- I am fearfully and wonderfully made. (Psalm 139:14)

My friend Michele Cushatt wrote *I Am,* a sixty-day devotional book, which is filled with biblical truths about who we are in Christ. Each entry helps us proclaim the truth about ourselves. I know many people who've found this practice, and this book, immensely helpful in their dark places. Just a few identities covered in the book are I Am: Wanted, Accepted, Known, Chosen, Treasured, Filled, Able, Called, Healed, Forgiven, and Comforted. If you're looking for a reminder of how God sees you, get a copy of this encouraging, truth-speaking book!

Claim the Armor

Around the time I launched my first book, a stranger started to harass me by phone. He somehow got access to my personal information and began to text, call, and leave voice messages of an extremely graphic nature. Even though I did all the earthly things we knew to do, like blocking phone numbers, enlisting prayer support from trusted friends, and consulting the authorities, it didn't stop. Each time I'd block a number, the perpetrator would wait a few days or weeks, choose a different phone number (purchased anonymously) and contact me again. I stopped answering my phone, but I lived in fear of a text popping up at any time.

It was paralyzing.

The harassment started in November, continued through the middle of January, and my book was due to release in February. Between Christmas and those few months being the busiest professional time I'd experienced to date, I was at the end of my rope. I'd been resistant to changing my phone number because I'd had it for over a decade; all my professional and personal contacts knew to find me that way. I just didn't want this creep to win by making me suffer because of his grievous behavior.

There are times when nothing else will do except claiming the armor of God. During that awful time, I prayed two things specifically. The first was Isaiah 54:17, which says, "No weapon forged against you will prevail."

The second Scripture I prayed speaks of the armor of God: "Put on every piece of God's armor so you will be able to resist the enemy in the time of evil. Then after the battle you will still be standing firm. Stand your ground, putting on the belt of truth and the body armor of God's righteousness. For shoes, put on the peace that comes from the Good News so that you will be fully prepared. In addition to all of these, hold up the shield of faith to stop the fiery arrows of the devil. Put on salvation as your helmet, and take the sword of the Spirit, which is the word of God." (Ephesians 6:13–17 NLT) Praying and focusing on God's armor reminded me that I wasn't fighting against the world; I was battling the enemy and the forces of darkness.

At one point, I decided I should also pray for this man who, if he was spending his time this way, was surely living in darkness. Admittedly, it took me months to get to this point, and I struggled to do it. But I do believe God wants us to pray for people who persecute us in any form.

The anxiety caused by wondering when I'd receive a call or text finally won out, so I changed my phone number and the harassment stopped. Several months later I found out that my harasser likely got my information from a speaker's website that listed my contact information and social media profiles. Turns out many women had reported similar experiences. After reporting it to the authorities, the website administrators also removed everyone's phone numbers from public view.

No doubt, the timing of this distraction wasn't a coincidence. And praying Scriptures served as a powerful reminder for me to stand firm in God's power, and not let the enemy derail me.

Pour Out Your Lament

I had the privilege of traveling to Israel with my husband in honor of our twenty-fifth wedding anniversary. One of the highlights of the trip for me was praying at the Western Wall in Jerusalem. The wall is a remnant of the border wall where both of Judaism's ancient temples once stood. Commonly called the "Wailing Wall," it's considered the most sacred spot in the Jewish religious tradition.

What struck me most was the heartfelt lament I could sense in the prayers of the Jewish people who were there. I didn't need to speak their language to understand the many cries full of pain, anguish, and pleading with God. It was a powerful reminder to me that we serve a holy, powerful God who isn't afraid of any prayer we bring Him. He's waiting with open ears and wants you to "Cast all your anxiety on Him, because He cares for you" (1 Peter 5:7).

God calls the book of Psalms worship. Yet there are plenty of psalms that are filled with lament. That means it's acceptable to express our heartfelt pain and sorrow to God. He's not afraid of your deepest, darkest pain. He can handle it and is not offended by your honesty.

My pastor friend Byron further enlightened me on the subject of lament. He told me that in the phrase "Blessed are those who mourn" found in Matthew 5:4, the word "mourn" actually means to lament. Mourn in this verse translated in Greek means, "get out what's inside you," or "to throw up, or out, what's inside." In other words, it's perfectly permissible to eject the sorrow, pain, and turmoil festering inside us. In fact, when we do we "will be comforted" (Matthew 5:4).

Even Jesus asked God, if it was possible, to take this cup (his crucifixion) from him. He wasn't afraid to ask his heavenly Father for what he wanted. We, like Jesus, can pray for God to change our circumstance. We can come boldly before the throne of grace with our heart's desires (Hebrews 4:16). We can pour out our pain, getting rid of what's eating us up inside.

 Praying a lament isn't a bad thing; it can be a holy form of worship.

Pray Differently

Not long ago, Dustin Woodward, my pastor, preached a sermon about prayer. In the midst of life's challenges, he suggested, "Sometimes, we have to go deeper and pray for something besides our circumstances." If you're feeling stuck in a place of despair, pity, fear, worry, or anxiety, there are many ways to pray. You can pray about God's character. Pray for others' needs. Pray through God's promises. Pray any prayer in the Bible where someone is praising God for who He is, not what He's done. Pray for all believers and the church as a whole.

Prayer centers me. It also helps me let go of the reins of control like no other practice. But I struggle to slow down my daily pace—especially in the middle of pressures and pain—to connect with God this way. I know prayer is good for me, but I often resist it. One way I combat this is to pray out loud instead of in my head. If I'm speaking my prayers, I'm less likely to fall asleep or get distracted (my weakness), and it's more like a conversation.

I also find that I can be more focused if I write down my prayers. Not only does this help me stay on point, it allows me to go back and see what I prayed for in the past. I can also see answered prayers more easily when they are written. Many people I know keep prayer journals where they list prayer requests or write out detailed prayers to God instead of offering them up in their head never to "see" them again. Journaling your prayers is a valuable way to pray differently if you're feeling like your prayer life is stagnant.

Ephesians 6:18 (NLT) says, "Pray in the Spirit at all times and on every occasion." And if you don't know what to pray, Romans 8:26 (ESV) says the Spirit intercedes on your behalf. "The Spirit helps us in our weakness. For we do not know what to pray for as we ought, but the Spirit himself intercedes for us with groanings too deep for words."

When Kelley was first diagnosed with leukemia, I organized a prayer meeting at our church. I was in charge, but I'd never led a prayer meeting like this before. The stakes were high because people were looking to me for wisdom, guidance, and encouragement. I had no idea what to pray for in the face of this crippling diagnosis.

Thankfully, I found the answer in Romans 8:26. I shared that verse and admitted to the crowd that I really didn't know what to pray, and it was okay if they didn't either because the Spirit had our back. I also shared the subsequent verses, which describe each of us as conquerors because of God's great love for us. We prayed for our sister using the powerful reminder that nothing can separate us from the love of God. No tribulation, distress, persecution, famine, nakedness, danger, or sword. Not death, life, angels, demons, the present, the future, or any powers. No height or depth or anything else in all creation (Romans 8:35–39 ESV).

And definitely not cancer, illness, abuse, anxiety, addiction, disease, divorce, infidelity, or homelessness. Not our performance or our lack thereof. Not our prayer life. Not our inability to follow without falling.

Nothing.

There's not a single thing we can put a name to that can separate us from God's vast, unwavering love for us.

When you're begging for breakthrough, ask the Spirit to shape your prayers. Pray in a different way, instead of praying the same thing with more intensity.

CHAPTER 16
Look for the Green

I will bless the Lord at all times;
His praise shall continually be in my mouth.
Psalm 34:1 ESV

Living in the High Desert for the last six years has taught me a few things. First, I've learned that there are seasons of brown, and seasons of "less brown." (Ha!) Not everyone has grass in their yard, but I wanted something green to look at in the midst of the dry, rocky landscape, so it was a prerequisite for me. Our backyard has a patch of grass that's roughly the size of a large in-ground swimming pool. Like in the Midwest, my grass is dormant in the winter months, even though it's not covered with snow. I anticipate April like I'm waiting for a new movie to come out, so excited am I that I'll have something beautiful to see when the grass comes to life again.

You might think this is a lot of hype for a small patch of grass, but if you've ever lived in the rocky terrain of a southwestern climate, you'd understand. When my grass is in its prime, from April through June (before the brown patches emerge from the intense heat of mid-summer), I savor my small sliver of solace. I often eat breakfast or enjoy my morning coffee there, as I watch the hummingbirds cavort among the flowering bushes and vines. I sway in the hammock, read my Bible, or stare at the majestic mountain nearby. The coolness of the watered grass brings welcome refreshment in comparison to the heat-filled rocks, pavement, and stucco walls that fill my yard and neighborhood.

My small patch of green fills me with gratitude. I've found my own slice of beauty in my desert.

Finding the Green

Some days, our lives feel like we're walking in the lush green hills of Ireland, and other days feel like we're trekking through the blazing sun of the Sahara Desert. In either scenario, we can choose our focus. We can obsess on the dry and weary ground, or we can look up for small signs of green—shifting our eyes to that which gives us hope and encouragement to press on. There are many sources of "green," and each is a step toward making gratitude part of our journey.

1. Past Provision

When my friends are facing a struggle with their kids, I like to remind them, "They won't always be wetting the bed, sleeping on the floor in your room, or sitting home alone on a Friday night." This serves as a powerful metaphor for our hardships; things will get better. His mercies are new every morning (Lamentations 3:22–23). Our present circumstance won't remain this way; progress will come in time.

Another way to find this form of gratitude is to dwell on what God has done for us in the past. The Israelites serve as a powerful reminder. Throughout the book of Exodus, God repeatedly delivered. From passage on dry ground through the Red Sea, to water from a rock, to quail and manna each day, to rules for living, God provided exactly what His people needed.

When you're in a dry place, look to the past.
Relish His provision—the means He used to see
you through to today.

He is faithful. Yet, we fall prey to the thinking "What have you done for me lately?" instead of "What amazing things you've done for me, God!" If our focus is on the daily bread we've already received, we can walk forward in faith and gratitude through our wilderness.

2. Daily Blessings

When Angie was in the desert of her cancer, a friend who had also battled breast cancer gave her a "blessings journal." Angie began detailing simple things to be thankful for each day. Counting her blessings, literally. And it changed her journey. She's told me countless times how helpful this one small gift was, then and now.

Now she mentors other parents of type 1 children and always gives that same gift to them when they hear the news. Angie says, "It seems counterintuitive to think of blessings in the midst of the greatest challenges of your life, but there's been no more important practice I've used to get me through them."

One Thousand Gifts by Ann Voskamp is a book based solely on the practice of gratitude. Born out of Voskamp's own personal struggles with loss and depression, it's a call to "celebrate grace and recognize the power of gratitude" in our lives. She even has an online community at www.onethousandgifts.com where readers are encouraged to share their own gifts of thanks.

Whether you read a book, keep a journal, or speak thanksgiving out loud, consider taking your own gratitude journey proclaiming God's provision, grace, and mercy. Even in the face of sorrow and anguish, there is always something for which to give thanks.

3. God's Unchanging Nature

The character and sovereignty of God are absolute. When it's hard to see green in the brown landscape of your life, try dwelling on the unchanging nature of God as a bedrock for your gratitude. The Bible says it like this: "Let us throw off everything that hinders and the sin that so easily entangles. And let us run with perseverance the race marked out for us, fixing our eyes on Jesus, the pioneer and perfecter of faith" (Hebrews 12:1–2). When we fix our eyes on the one who made all things and finishes all things, we can be grateful that we don't have to carry the weight of the world. Nor do we have to have all the answers.

If you're stuck, try starting with this prayer:

"God, thank you that you hold the universe in your hands. Thank you for loving me exactly how I am, and for who I am. I praise you that you are always the same, yesterday, today, and forever. I'm grateful for your Word that is trustworthy and never goes out or returns empty. I acknowledge the futility of my attempts at control. I want to walk in your ways. I want to praise you for who you are, not just what you've done or given to me. I will give thanksgiving in all circumstances, doing my best to continually give you praise. Let me glorify you, despite how I feel. Multiply my faith and trust in you, God, as there are days I feel my faith is smaller than a mustard seed. You aren't stumped by my questions; you aren't thwarted by my doubts. You are seated on a throne, holy, powerful, loving, and almighty. I honor and revere you. And I'm above all grateful you call me yours. Amen."

You can also spark your thanksgiving with these trusted truths about God:

- God is the same yesterday, today, and forever. (Hebrews 13:8)
- God is an ever-present help. (Psalm 46:1)
- God's Word never goes out empty. (Isaiah 55:11)
- God accomplishes His purposes. (Isaiah 46:10)
- Nothing can be added to or taken away from what God's done. (Ecclesiastes 3:14)
- God's grace is sufficient. (2 Corinthians 12:9)
- God is the finisher of our faith. (Hebrews 12:2 KJV)
- God is holy. (Isaiah 6:3)
- God is sovereign. (Daniel 4:35)
- God is trustworthy. (Psalm 9:10)
- God is near to the brokenhearted. (Psalm 34:18)
- God saves us. (Acts 4:12)

4. Blooms in the Desert

While she walks through chronic illness and other struggles, Laura focuses on this text from Philippians 4:8–9: "Whatever is true, whatever is noble, whatever is right, whatever is pure, whatever is lovely, whatever is admirable—if anything is excellent or praiseworthy—think about such things. Whatever you have learned or received or heard from me, or seen in me—put it into practice. And the God of peace will be with you." I think about each of these attributes in this passage as blooms on a cactus. Even though the cactus is filled with thorny spines, the flowers still adorn the plant with beauty.

I've led mission trips to Haiti for almost a decade. I've seen all manner of horrific conditions, human frailty, death, and destitution. We deliver water regularly in an area named Cité Soleil. Homes often consist of tin walls and tarp roofs. A "nice" home has cinder-block walls and mud floors. In developed countries, we'd call this a slum.

At first glance, the faces of the naked, hungry children take your breath away. However, upon deeper examination, one sees beauty under the surface. Cité Soleil has taught me to replace my sorrow with gratitude. Not just gratitude for all that my white American privileges afford me. But also, gratitude to witness the beauty of Haiti's people.

I'm grateful for the children whose pure eyes beam with affection for me, despite our differences. I'm grateful to watch the lovely hands of a brother as he bathes his younger siblings in the middle of the street. I'm grateful to carry water alongside the admirable mother who is working hard to support her family. I'm grateful for the praiseworthy hearts of the children who sing of God's goodness in the middle of a garbage dump. I'm grateful for the excellence of the organization I serve with, whose heart is to create jobs, strengthen families, and lift people out of their poverty.

In situations or seasons of plenty, it's easy for our hearts to blossom with gratitude. But in the worst circumstances imaginable, we can still focus our attention on that which is true, lovely, pure, and admirable.

As we navigate the difficult terrain of our trials, gratitude can come from many sources.

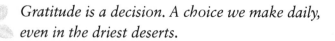

Gratitude is a decision. A choice we make daily, even in the driest deserts.

You won't always make the perfect choice to be thankful in all things, nor is your gratitude an insurance policy. But it's a worthy place to direct your efforts, whenever possible, so you can thrive in the middle of your "Sahara."

Sometimes, a sliver of green is all we need to keep us going.

CHAPTER 17

Tend Your Soil

The angel of the Lord encamps around those who fear him,
and he delivers them.

Psalm 34:7

After Kelley died of leukemia, I pretended I was okay. It seemed to me that I had to suck it up because others had more "right" to grieve than me because I wasn't a family member. I started to feel the ill effects of my sorrow, only I didn't ask for help. After about nine months, I landed in the emergency room with heart attack symptoms. Following an overnight stay and a full work-up, which showed no signs of heart trouble, the doctors determined my symptoms were related to stress and deemed it an anxiety attack. I wasn't "getting over" losing my friend.

Five years of walking alongside Kelley through her illness took a physical and mental toll on me. I had been stuffing my sorrow and caring for everyone but myself. My husband and a dear friend sat me down and encouraged me to seek help.

Why does it always have to be so terrible before we get help? (And even if our health is suffering, we don't always get the help we need.) We covered anxiety and depression in chapter 9 but those aren't the only ramifications we face in trials. That's why we're going to address the important subject of self-care in this chapter.

"Self-care" is a phrase that elicits mixed reactions. For some people, these words don't come with a negative connotation, and they're happy to be given any permission to take care of themselves in the middle of their crisis. For others, there's baggage that comes with this phrase. Maybe even resentment for the people who continually beg them to "take care of yourself," or over the fact that they don't feel they have the time they need to do that right now. Possibly, you're carrying a suitcase of guilt that prevents you from considering self-care an option. Or maybe you're like me, and you don't like being told what to do.

Wherever you stand out on this subject, it must be addressed. What's a book about surviving when your world is out of control without some guidelines for how to take back control of your life? In this chapter, we'll cover caring for your soul, heart, body, and mind, and practical ways to do so.

One important disclaimer before we move on comes from my wise friend Patricia who said, "Don't get fooled by words like 'don't forget to take care of yourself,' or 'you have to put up boundaries with your loved one.' That *may* be the case; however, it may *not* be. It's simply a judgment. I will never regret each moment I gave to my mom and dad. It was over so quickly, and there is a vast time afterward to recover your senses. It's a tough call. For me, those worn-out pieces of advice were annoying. This was my crisis. I wasn't particularly looking for a way out. I was looking for a way to put more energy into it, not less. I was looking for acceptance for how I needed to spend my energy."

No matter which camp you've pitched your tent in, I guarantee you'll find something useful here if you're willing to keep an open mind. It's important you take an honest inventory of how you are caring for yourself. Are you already getting what you need? Or do you need to make some changes, so you can get through this in one piece?

Your well-being matters; don't neglect it.

Rx for Your Soul

First on the list of self-care is tending to your soul. My friend Byron is not only a colleague but a dear friend. He's been ministering to God's flock in one form or another for over thirty-five years. And he's faced his own adversity. Most recently, his wife had emergency surgery for a detached retina in her left eye. Shockingly enough, within twelve hours of her first surgery, Byron had a stroke in his left eye. Despite further surgery and continued care, they are both now virtually blind in their left eyes. Byron jokes that without depth perception, they often collide around the house!

When I asked Byron what he did to get through his hard place, I couldn't type fast enough to catch all the wisdom he shared. What follows is his prescription for facing hardship. And it's pure gold.

1. Listen to God.

Both Psalm 46:10 and Exodus 14:14 encourage us to be still, listen, and let God do His work. Byron says, "When I had my double foot surgery where I was sedentary for six weeks, I had more time for solitude than I'd had for twenty years! I learned that solitude and listening to God was the foundation of processing and praying about my hardship. In this newest trial, both my wife and I have spent time doing this. This practice is essential for us."

2. Be Honest with Trusted Friends.

Byron suggests that it's important to vent to people we know we can trust. "We have four couples in our small group to whom we can sound off. There's no judgment, no trying to fix it. They just pray, listen, and encourage us." If you don't have these traveling buddies, I can't emphasize enough the importance of finding and confiding in people who won't judge you. Being honest when things are hard doesn't mean you lack faith; it just means you need to get it out, so you can try to move on. These trusted confidantes, whether family or friends, are critical to journeying well.

3. Trust God without Any Expectations.

For Byron, this means "trusting God without having to know why or that something else good will happen." He clings to the truth found in Colossians 2:6–7 and reminds us to receive Romans 11:33–36 so we can stay focused on who God is and to be totally surrendered to His will. Byron says, "God is God, I belong to Him, and I am free when I totally surrender. Who are we to think we should give counsel to God? His ways are above our ways. Everything comes from Him and by His power."

4. Choose Joy.

Byron says, "My wife and I remind each other that we are choosing to choose joy today. It's important for us to verbalize this regularly."

There's a difference between joy and happiness. Joy is a way of life; happiness deals just with circumstances.

As we discussed in chapter 6, mindset is critical and helps us navigate the troubled times with clarity. Maybe joy won't be your focus, but whatever your focal point, remind yourself often, even out loud, so you stay on track.

5. Spend regular time in God's Word.

No prescription for soul care is complete without the addition of routine time in God's Word. Reading God's Word and/or studying it with a group of people helps us to keep our hearts in touch with God. If you're feeling stuck with one method for connection, remember to try another approach instead of trying harder. Online sermons, podcasts, music, devotionals, Bible study, church, and small groups are all ways to care for your soul. When you're facing adversity, don't give up this practice of being with God, in the company of others or alone. It's paramount to self-care.

Body Care

The garden of your soul needs tending, but the physical part of your body needs attention too. Many respondents and friends said the one thing they maintained in times of crisis was their regular exercise routine. Maybe you have to cut down how often, but don't cut out your exercise completely. Even my friend Kelley had a treadmill brought into her tiny germ-proof room after her bone marrow transplant, so she could keep her body as strong as possible. Despite how sick she was, she tried to walk a tiny bit each day. Her physical strength and stamina were nonnegotiable.

Patricia faithfully kept her practice of yoga throughout her several-year journey of caring for her elderly parents. Pam considers her walking time sacred as she cares for the daily needs of her mother, who's facing dementia in a nursing home.

There are many options to care for your body, whether they are cosmetic or physical. Each is important. Try yoga, Pilates, walking, running, weight lifting, biking, swimming, hiking, baths, pedicures, haircuts and colors, and so on. Whatever you choose, it's an important part of tending to your physical body.

Maybe you just need an outlet for your stress that isn't neces-sarily a form of exercise. Try scrapbooking, cooking, knitting, time with friends, reading, television, sitting by a lake or stream, garden-ing, or anything else that relaxes and restores you.

Exercise and diet go hand in hand. How you fuel your body is equally important. When times are rough or I'm in crisis mode, I struggle to stay on the no-carb bus. For me, this only compounds my lethargic tendencies. Each of us gets to decide what foods make us feel better, of course, but pay attention to what you're putting into your body. Making intentional choices about what you eat can be a critical way to keep some control in an out-of-control situa-tion. You get to choose, so whether that's comfort food or a rigid diet plan, it's up to you.

Bottom line: When we feel better physically, we *feel* better in other ways too.

Mind Care

My friend Karen L. says this all the time: "I try to remember what's God's job and what's my job." This mindset has helped her withstand over a decade of chronic leukemia treatments, two sepa-rate breast cancer diagnoses, and resultant surgeries. Karen focuses on prayer, scheduling and attending doctor appointments even when she's hesitant, eating right, exercising, community involve-ment, and choosing joy. And she lets God do the rest.

So, what belongs in your job description? Following are a few ways you can care for your mind that will keep you sane during your trial.

1. Choose Your Battles.

Isaiah 54:17 says, "No weapon forged against you will prevail." When we are in the hard place, it's easy to let people's comments, slights, or behavior get to us. People will say lots of frustrating things, like calling your cancer or grief a "journey." (Even I did that through this whole book. Sorry!) It's important to prioritize what you want to spend your brain time on, so you can save your energy. Don't sweat the small stuff and decide which battles are important to fight.

When it comes to friends and family, you'll possibly face what might feel like betrayal, or people who say or do the wrong thing. Each of these grievances are difficult; however, many times they can be attributed to unmet expectations.

First, consider the Relationship Tier, and then determine if it's important enough to confront someone about their words or actions. If it's a Tier 1 or 2 person, you might have to have a conversation, but perhaps if a Tier 3 or 4 acquaintance doesn't behave the way you'd like, you will decide to let it go.

Consider the end game. Ask yourself, "Would I be sad if this person was out of my life after my trial is over? Or do I think this relationship is important enough to fight for?" These questions help focus your thoughts in the direction of desired outcomes, as opposed to your immediate feelings. They might guide you toward grace for yourself or others to preserve necessary relationships. Or they might allow you the freedom to let go of people who aren't filling the needs you have, not just now, but in general. Filter every decision through a lens of grace.

If words have hurt you, first consider the source. Is this friend or family member characterized by saying the wrong thing or lacking tact? Don't expect more of them now; a zebra is unlikely to change its stripes during a hard time. Second, consider if there is any truth in the words they spoke to you. If there is a kernel of truth, try to allow it to penetrate your mind for your benefit. Sometimes, even if someone isn't eloquent or kind, they are getting to the root of something we need to hear. After filtering it through the lens of self-examination and what God says about it, take what you need, and leave the rest.

Did someone disappoint you by not being there for you? I've seen both sides of this: people in crisis who feel left behind by their friends and friends who feel left behind by the person in crisis. Again, look at the big picture and ask yourself if you value this friendship enough to let the hurt go. And also, be sure to ask yourself if you owe anyone an apology. Don't compound your trial by sacrificing valued friends and family members because you chose the wrong battle.

2. Give Yourself Permission.

Even if you won't give yourself permission, here's a healthy dose from me! You deserve rest. You deserve to be kind to yourself. You deserve to have a break, to hit the pause button. You can say no to the things that don't fill you up. It's okay to do what makes you healthy right now.

The world will not stop spinning on its axis if you aren't there to hold it up.

If this is too hard for you, start by asking yourself these questions:

- If I wasn't in the middle of this right now, what would I be telling myself to do to take care of myself? (Hint: Do that.)
- How can I be sure I don't fall apart?
- What can I do to care for myself so that I can keep doing _____?
- What would I tell my friend or loved one in the same situation? (Say the same thing to yourself.)
- What do I know now that I didn't know when this began? Should I change my actions because of that?

In the middle of your trial isn't the place to beat yourself up about the things you should be doing or not doing. With her relationship and therapy clients, Susie Albert Miller uses this phrase often: "Stop 'should-ing' all over yourself!" If you need to watch a movie and eat popcorn with your kids today instead of conquering that to-do list, so be it. If you need to skip that party or those errands to rest, do it. If you must work out today, no matter what else falls to the wayside, let the rest go and work out. If you can't imagine getting out of bed because your body is screaming at you, stay in bed. If you need to cry or set up an appointment with a counselor, get on the phone. If you need time with a trusted friend, schedule it.

We fight the battle in our minds when we believe lies like, "I'm not enough," "I can't do what I want," or "I should be doing something." When you begin to play that recording full of untruths, hit the stop button, rewind, and start again.

 Tell yourself that the way things are now won't last forever and that you have permission to do what you need to do, for you, for today.

3. Do the Next Thing.

Sometimes, your feelings won't match your faith. If you're at the end of your rope, do only what you need to get through today. There will be times when you'll be living second to second, minute to minute, or day by day. That's perfectly acceptable! If you need to narrow your focus, permission granted. If you need to process your anxiety, grief, frustration, anguish, or guilt with someone, do it! (You can always schedule a paid therapy appointment.) If you need accountability, ask a friend or family member to help you by checking in on you. The end justifies the means.

This is your climb, and you can take as many baby steps as you need to get where you're going.

But don't give up. For now, put one foot on the ground, get out of bed, cook that meal, drive that child, go to your doctor appointment, get to that next break at work, take that one small action, make that phone call. You've got this! You will get there! I promise the path won't always look this dim; the light is coming. And someday you'll look back at this time in your life and say, "I got through that. Yay, me!"

Self-care can be tricky, but we can't neglect this important aspect of our trial. The only rule is: You get to make the rules—as long as you've been open-minded and intentional about assessing how you're *really* doing. I care about you, and I want you to do whatever you can to improve your situation, even if it's just a fraction. No more excuses; you've got plenty of ammunition.

CHAPTER 18
Remove the Boulders

Whether you turn to the right or to the left,
your ears will hear a voice behind you, saying,
"This is the way; walk in it."

Isaiah 30:21

The Sandia Mountains near my home are covered with majestic boulders. From afar they appear like dots on a tapestry; up close they resemble giants. We love to capture photos of the breathtaking vistas from atop the highest rocks during our hikes. And our favorite picnic perch is affectionately call "lunch rock."

Boulders can be good or bad, depending how we view them. They can offer either a welcome vantage point or a barrier to our path. They can be a sheltered place to sleep or an insurmountable precipice to climb. They can be a resting place or a heavy weight that can't be lifted.

How will you see the boulders in your journey? Will you climb on top of them so you can see things more clearly? Or will you be thwarted because you can't see your way around them? Will you be protected by their mass? Or oblivious to their presence? Or will you find a way to remove them so you can walk freely again?

Confronting the Boulders

Boulders can be a friendly part of the landscape of our lives, but if we're not mindful, they can also tumble out of nowhere and crush us. When you're in a trial, it's easy to miss the boulders that stand in the way of your health, freedom, and welfare. Several boulders have the potential to thwart your journey. We'll cover four of them, the first of which is the boulder of unmet expectations.

Unmet Expectations

Expectations can get us into trouble. The standard we set for ourselves, others, and even God often can't be met. In the dry and weary land of our trial, something has to give. If we keep setting unreachable expectations, we will continue to be disappointed. Three types of expectations deserve our attention.

1. Expectations of Ourselves

Susie Albert Miller speaks to the unhealthy expectations we can place on ourselves during a crisis. She says, "Beware of what story you're telling yourself about what you should or shouldn't be doing! Oftentimes, this story comes from our youth, and it says we should pray more, go to church more, believe more, and so on. But there's no should; there's just struggle." It's unrealistic to expect ourselves to do everything we normally do, especially in the middle of a trial, or that there is a right thing to do.

We weigh ourselves down with "shoulds." If you're grieving, you tell yourself, "I should be able to go thirty minutes without crying." If you've got cancer, you tell yourself, "I should be able to get out of bed and take care of my kids." If you're suffering from depression, you tell yourself, "I should be able to pray and not have to take medication." If you're facing divorce or separation, you tell yourself, "I shouldn't be lonely." If you're struggling with a wayward child, you tell yourself, "I should have been a better mom."

All of these "shoulds" are lies. You already learned to stop "should-ing" all over yourself. It's important to take care of yourself, not beat yourself up. Don't place insurmountable expectations on yourself. Feel your feelings and do what you need to do. Allow yourself time to sit in your pain and just be. When you stop playing the "should" recording, you'll be able focus on what you really need instead of what you think you should need.

Another way to manage expectations of yourself, your home, or your life is to "let go of the how, for now." This requires relinquishing control, which is hard to do! But if you focus on the end result, as opposed to the means it takes to get there, you'll save a lot of energy for other, more pressing matters.

2. Expectations of Others

People will make mistakes as they walk alongside you in your hard place. We can't expect them to navigate our terrain perfectly when we can hardly find our own way! You can save yourself a lot of heartache if you lower your expectations and focus on communicating your needs instead.

Garrett Wilk, a licensed professional counselor who works with adult mental health patients, says, "Telling people how they can be there for you relieves people of the imperative to give you advice. It also allows them to help you." If you have a hard time verbalizing what you need or don't need, Wilk suggests a three-prong approach: a) state the problem, b) tell them how you feel, and c) give them another option. This approach is especially useful for Tier 1 and 2 relationships. The more contact you have with someone, the greater the need is for clear communication of your needs.

To flesh this out in real life, let's return to our example from earlier in the book where a woman with cancer was struggling with her sister.

Her sister's negative emotions and fear regarding her cancer were affecting this woman's emotional and physical well-being. She handled this situation with her sister beautifully. She spoke assertively, set guidelines, and stated her feelings. If we were to put her words into Wilk's three-prong approach. she could say this to her sister: "I can't handle your stress and anxiety about my cancer; it's standing in the way of my care and healing. Your strong emotions and negative outlook make me feel like I have to take care of you, instead of worrying about myself. If you want to come and visit me, I need you to control your emotions and provide encouragement for me."

No one will be perfect in how they show love or show up for you in your hard times. Your job is to be honest with your feelings and what you need. Wilk says, "Effective communication isn't a one-and-done proposition. Don't set the expectation that someone will do it right the first time. There will be trial and error, and you will both make mistakes. But remember, you are each entitled to your own emotions, and you don't need to fix those emotions."

You can also reset your expectation barometer by focusing on the good, not the bad, in others. If you expect people to do their best, you will find the positive in what they do or say. If you are watching and waiting for them to fail you in one way or another, you will most certainly find their faults. Try to forgive people who fall short or can't give you what you need. And remember, you're not perfect either.

3. Expectations of God

In the last chapter, we learned about Byron's Rx for the soul. One of the keys in his prescription was to trust God without expectations—without having to know why or that something else good will happen in the future. This gave me pause.

I'm guilty of placing unrealistic expectations on God about my happiness, my physical health, my family's health, my finances, my future. When He doesn't meet my expectations, my faith falters. I want the kind of faith where I trust God no matter what comes my way. I don't want to wonder why He didn't give me something or why He took something away. I want my expectation of God to always be aligned with the Bible and what it says about God's unchanging character and His vast love for me.

Byron said, "When I lost my eyesight, I thought, 'This is unfair when I have so much to do and you've given me so much responsibility, God.' But I decided I was going to live each day by what I know to be true about God. Things like He's always faithful, His mercies are new every morning, He has the best plan for me, and He gives me comfort so that I can comfort others." Byron is committed to living out this truth in his life. He challenges himself to maintain this attitude daily: "God, today I'm going to give everything I know about myself to everything I know about you."

When we align our expectations around who God is, not what He does or doesn't do for us, we can walk freely in the right direction without a boulder blocking our path.

Unacknowledged Denial

Maybe you've been in your hard place for a long time, and you've come to a place of acceptance. Or maybe you're still coming to terms with your new reality. Ironically, if you're in denial, it can be hard to see this boulder. Either way, it's important to take an honest inventory of your current situation so this boulder doesn't threaten your well-being.

Death of a loved one isn't the only thing we grieve in our lives. Trials like cancer, divorce, unemployment, natural disasters, chronic illness, post-traumatic stress disorder, and many others involve grief as well. Although the grief process isn't always linear, denial is considered the first stage of grief. Denial and shock go hand in hand and are part of the numbness we feel after a significant loss or life change. Inherently, shock and denial are good. They help us cope and make survival possible.

To move out of denial, you have to experience the shock of what's happened to you. This can be difficult and, sometimes, we resist this part of the process because sitting in the pain can be uncomfortable. Stephanie Porter, licensed marriage and family therapist, says, "Denial and shock have purpose, but they also have an expiration date!" Left unchecked, denial leads us straight into fear. Fear intensifies denial's hold on us and keeps us from moving forward toward healing.

To illustrate, let's say your spouse is diagnosed with a severe, life-threatening illness. Initially, you might look for any other reality except the one you're living. You are in shock about this diagnosis, and denial quickly follows. The reason you might remain in denial is that you are afraid of losing your spouse or you don't want to experience the negative ramifications of your new reality. This results in all your future decisions being clouded by your new lens of fear. We resist facing our denial because we don't want to experience the fear.

It's a vicious circle. Denial, shock, and fear keep us from resolving our intense emotions. These emotions will keep us trapped, and their weight will eventually crush us. While denial is an important stepping stone in grieving your previous "normal," you can't let it spiral into paralyzing fear.

Unwarranted Fear

We can have fearful episodes, or bad days, when our fear wreaks havoc with our best intentions. But if we continuously operate in fear, we deny our faith in God's provision. And if we don't trust God, the boulder of perpetual fear will eventually roll down and crush us.

Are you living in fear of your cancer returning? Are you living in fear of your husband's addiction wreaking havoc on your life again? Are you afraid your kids won't turn out okay because you got divorced? Are you afraid you won't be able to stand up under the overwhelming grief you're experiencing? Are you fearful of what people will think if they find out the truth about you? Are you fearful that your kids will never get their life back on track?

The Bible says God's "perfect love drives out fear" (1 John 4:18) and that "God gave us a spirit not of fear but of power and love and self-control" (2 Timothy 1:7 ESV).

God grants us a spirit of power and love so we can bring our fear under control. His love for us is the remedy to fear.

If we believe the Bible and take God at His word, our fear is unfounded. There are hundreds of verses in the Bible that include the phrases "fear not" or "be not afraid." God is serious about us trusting Him and not worrying about the "what-ifs" in life.

We can combat our fear by speaking out loud the truth of God's provision. This verse is a great place to start: "Fear not, (*insert your name*), for I am with you; be not dismayed, for I am your God; I will strengthen you, I will help you, I will uphold you with my righteous right hand" (Isaiah 41:10 ESV). When we stand upon the rock of God's great love for us, we can conquer the fear that threatens our faith.

Unforgiveness

My husband, Craig, loves to mountain bike on a rocky trail near our home. While biking one night, he braked hard to avoid a big boulder and flew off his bike. He landed smack dab in the middle of a cactus! He came home with hands and legs full of small spines and tried to pull them out one by one with tweezers. Some he could see to remove; others were too small. Within days, the remaining minuscule slivers of cactus became small, infected sores.

And like that cactus, people might hurt you in your hard place, leaving minuscule "slivers" that won't heal. Friends might say and do things that are stupid, insensitive, and unkind. Family members may overstep their bounds. Loved ones might dishonor your relationship. Some of them knowingly, others oblivious to the collateral damage they've inflicted.

These wounds are painful. And your feelings of frustration and anger are normal.

 But unforgiveness, left untreated, will infect our hearts and minds.

Many years ago, a close friend from church wounded me with words. I bore responsibility in this situation, too, but I struggled to let go of her words. And even though we both said we were sorry and asked for forgiveness, I still harbored anger. For months, I replayed the conversation in my mind, and it wreaked havoc on my mental and physical health. I had to find a way to move past this hurt so bitterness and resentment wouldn't infect my heart and mind.

Finally, I spent time with God, assessing what was "mine" to learn from and what was not mine to carry. I poured out all my anger, sorrow, and frustration in a letter to my friend—which I never intended to send. Then I prayed over it, asking God to help me forgive her and to release me from my incessant anguish. When I was finished, I burned the letter in the fireplace. For the first time in months, I felt relief from the unrelenting burden.

Afterwards, I had to make a conscious choice to do the hard work required to remain friends. No doubt, I was guarded. I'm sure she felt it, wondering if I'd truly forgiven her. But we pressed on because the friendship mattered—even if things were different. After I moved away, the distance helped create space for healing. We continued to spend time together when we visited and, at some undefined point, I stopped remembering the pain we had caused each other.

We'd found our way to a renewed friendship.

If you're struggling with a hurt, face your unforgiveness head-on. Get those tweezers and dig out the painful words and actions of others and cleanse your mind of the wrongs. Keep showing up, being honest, and doing the hard things instead of hanging out in the wasteland of bitterness. Once you remove the unforgiveness, there is room for healing. God wired not just our bodies but our spirits to regenerate, heal, and grow new life where pain once resided.

And just like my friendship, God can redeem what once felt lost.

Hebrews 12:14–15 (NLT) says, "Work at living in peace with everyone, and work at living a holy life. ... Watch out that no poisonous root of bitterness grows up to trouble you, corrupting many." You can't change someone else, but you can change your-self. So, as far as it depends on you, your job is to live at peace with others and not let unforgiveness fester. Recognize that even small slivers of pain have the potential to become bigger wounds if you're not careful.

Relationships require effort, humility, and forgiveness. We are all deserving of forgiveness and should ask for and give it freely. Even if we've said the words "I forgive you," we need to be diligent about working to align our heart with our words. If you don't think you can do it on your own, ask God for help. He's in the business of healing the broken, mending the wounds, and making things new.

And when you offer forgiveness to those who've hurt you along the way, your boulder will become a place of beauty instead of a barrier.

Forgiving Yourself

Perhaps your hard place is due to a mistake you've made. Forgiving yourself is another monumental boulder you'll have to move if you want to be whole and healed. Maybe you had an affair, which caused a marriage crisis, separation, or divorce. Maybe you've struggled with addiction resulting in adverse effects to you or others. Maybe you failed to follow through on something and now you're paying the price. Maybe your past has finally caught up with you. Maybe you wounded a friend. Maybe you haven't been able to keep all those promises you've made to God and others.

Our wayward behavior, or sin, will have consequences. And yours could be the cause of the predicament you're in right now. This can be hard to reconcile, and you might be justified in your anger toward yourself. But you can't stay there. It's essential to forgive yourself and release your guilt. Kay Woodward, another of my pastors, says, "Let go of anything that says you aren't 100 percent worthy, lovely, and wonderful!"

It's your choice. You can stay mired in the muck of self-deprecation and unforgiveness, or you can accept God's grace and be forgiven.

 No matter how dirty your yesterday, God is willing to grant you a shiny, new future.

Ephesians 2:4–5 says, "Because of His great love for us, God, who is rich in mercy, made us alive with Christ even when we were dead in transgressions—it is by grace you have been saved." The first time I read those verses, something changed inside me. I

gained a new understanding of the gift God offers me—the grace of undeserved forgiveness. Unconditional love. Freedom from striving. Unearned favor.

Even when we make a mess of our lives, He's waiting to clean us up and accept us where we are, just as we are. And He offers this freely, unbiased by our past performance. Without promise of our ability to be perfect in the future. Oh, the extravagant grace of Jesus!

Friend, I don't know where you are today. Maybe you're a lifelong follower of Christ who is struggling to believe that you can forgive yourself for what you've done. Or maybe you're someone who doesn't understand the concept of a loving Father who accepts you with open arms regardless of your mistakes. Or maybe you've never claimed faith of your own before, but you're drawn to God's message of grace through Jesus.

But where you're at or where you've been isn't as important as where God wants to take you. What matters most is this: Nothing can separate us from the love of God (Romans 8:35–39). And God, through His son Jesus' sacrifice on the cross, is ready to accept you, forgive you, and welcome you into His kingdom. Don't wait another second to take this step of faith.

When you confess your past transgressions, accept what he did for you on the cross, and ask him to take over, God will grant you a new future.

And regardless of the hardship you're facing right now, He will put a new song in your mouth.

Part 4:

Destination

*Because of the Lord's great
love we are not consumed,
for His compassions never fail.
They are new every morning;
great is your faithfulness.*

Lamentations 3:22-23

CHAPTER 19

Hard but Holy

After you have suffered a little while,
the God of all grace,
who has called you to His eternal glory in Christ,
will Himself restore, confirm, strengthen,
and establish you.

1 Peter 5:10 ESV

Her name was Brenda.

She had terminal cancer and, during her short battle with this reprehensible enemy, we rallied around her, prayed fervently for healing, and ministered to her needs in a variety of ways. As her death loomed close, I remember a certain day with crystal clarity. My pastor had just returned from visiting her and I asked him how the visit went. His response caught me off guard, "It was beautiful. I feel privileged every time I get to be part of the end of someone's life."

"Beautiful?" I was perplexed. How can someone dying be beautiful?

When my brother Dan died, I wasn't walking closely with God. I was devastated. I didn't feel peace or hope, I just felt that death robbed me of one of my favorite people on earth (which is true).

When my dad died, it was easier somehow, possibly because my dad was in his mid-seventies and had endured his share of pain. Dan, on the other hand, died instantly of a heart attack in his early forties. But I think the real difference between the two was that I was seeing death through a lens of faith instead of loss.

My pastor's words that day became a catalyst for me and sparked my reframed view of death and dying. I began to see how death could be special, precious, and holy. And I didn't cling to this earthly life as the only thing that mattered.

Little did I know that, in the years to come, I'd become intimately acquainted with the holiness that comes in the days, hours, and minutes as life draws to a close. I now also consider it a privilege to be invited into the intimate space at the end of a life.

It's a rare opportunity to tread on sacred ground, even if it's hard. Ecclesiastes 3:20 (ESV) says, "All go to one place. All are from the dust, and to dust all return." Death will come to us all. But we get to decide if we'll be paralyzed by its presence or behold its potential.

Finishing Well

If you or someone you love is facing a terminal diagnosis, imagine my arms reaching across the page to give you a tender embrace. I've been in the inner sanctuary of many terminally ill loved ones, and it's never easy. But I pray that you would receive what I'm about to say with the humility and love I feel as I write it.

I do believe we can finish well.

As you, or someone who loves you, reads this, I pray that you'll cherish the hard but holy ground that comes with the end of life. I've witnessed those who cling to life and never relent. And I've watched as families allow dying to be a meaningful process ... an exclamation point on a life well lived.

You get to choose. You can finish well, or you can hold tightly to something that was never intended to be fully within our grasp.

Everyone will walk this road differently; you will know what finishing well looks like for you. The only rule is you get to make the rules.

Now is not the time to caretake for everyone around you. Be clear with those you love about what it is you need or want. Don't let fear rob you of the clarity and closure you need. If you have unfinished business, handle it. If there's a conversation you need to have, have it. If there's an apology that needs to be made, make it. If there's forgiveness you need to offer, offer it. If there are letters that need writing, write them. If there are plans to be made, make them. If there's someone you want to see, see them. If there are possessions that need giving away, give them. If you want to talk about dying, talk about it. If you don't want to talk about dying, don't. If there's grace that needs offering, offer it.

Your legacy matters. Do what you need to leave it intact.

If it's not you but your loved one who's dying, consider reading this chapter to them as a means to open dialogue about finishing well. Take the above words to heart and give loads of permission and grace to the person who's preparing to leave this earth. Your new role is to come alongside. To support and care for and tend to the needs of the person you love. The little things don't matter right now. Ask your loved one what they want or need. Give them control where possible. Choose your battles. Give them plenty of space to process their grief. Help them carve out the margin they need to do what's important to them—even if that isn't what *you* need.

Your time to heal will be later. Their time is now. Don't waste it or wish it away. Help them finish well. It's the greatest gift you can give.

Even If

We met Keith and Kassandra when we were speaking at a marriage retreat. We'd spied them throughout the weekend, whispering intently with friends during our sessions, or staring adoringly into each other's eyes while two-stepping on the dance floor. It was hard not to miss him with his stately cowboy hat, her with her sly smile and simple beauty. It was clear they were madly in love.

We were surprised when the organizers of the retreat asked us to pray for them after our last session. What would they need prayer for? On the outside they appeared confident and in love.

That wasn't the problem.

We quickly unraveled the mystery, much to our dismay. Keith, a police officer at the time, had been charged with the second-degree murder of a man he killed in the line of duty. The trial and jury selection were to happen the next day. After years of waiting, wondering, and putting their future on hold, their time had come. Their future would soon be decided.

That prayer on a Sunday morning several years ago was the beginning of our friendship with Keith and Kassandra.

The couple had only been married two years when the trial began. Faithful family and friends stood by them, raised money for their legal defense fund, prayed for them, and supported them in countless ways. Their supporters encouraged them through social media as well and they created their own hashtag—#sandystrong. Keith and Kassandra are forever grateful to those who walked alongside them in the dark valley of those four and a half years.

But many others vilified them. Before, during, and after the trial, their names were constantly in the media, and they were harshly criticized by protesters, strangers, and even "friends." They faced scrutiny, death threats, and condemnation everywhere they turned. People called Keith "a hateful killing machine," never accounting for the risks he took, the people he saved, the criminals he caught, or the sex trafficking he thwarted in his twenty-year career.

In the throes of the trial and ensuing chaos, it was tempting to give up hope. Kassandra said, "We had all these mountains in front of us: finance, legal, conflict, emotions, change, media, relationship tensions. But we couldn't let the hopelessness win. We had to choose to move forward every day. We started small, taking one step at a time."

All that hate and negativity could have taken them out but, instead, it caused them to draw nearer to God and trust His plan more than ever before. They dove deep into their faith. They attended church and started to serve the community there. They read and studied the Bible. They memorized Scripture. Keith even carried Scripture cards in his chest pocket, close to his heart, every day during the trial.

In all of it, they clung to God.

This was the Scripture verse they chose as their focus: "Through Him we have also obtained access by faith into this grace in which we stand, and we rejoice in hope of the glory of God. Not only that, but we rejoice in our sufferings, knowing that suffering produces endurance, and endurance produces character, and character produces hope, and hope does not put us to shame, because God's love has been poured into our hearts through the Holy Spirit who has been given to us" (Romans 5:2–5 ESV).

A hung jury led to Keith's acquittal. But it was months later before they received word that there would not be a retrial. Keith was finally free.

But his freedom didn't come from a court, a judge, a lawyer, or a favorable ruling. His true freedom came as a result of standing in faith, with unwavering hope in God's love, and by accepting the grace of Jesus that was poured out for him.

He was able to stand through it all because faith does not disappoint.

In the heart of the storm, Kassandra had her doubts. She was trying to figure out how she would care for and provide for her family if Keith went to jail. Her thoughts were consumed by this notion, every action a symptom of her fear of her husband's potential, horrifying fate.

During the height of her stress and anxiety over her family's future, a woman spoke this truth into Kassandra's life: "Even if Keith goes to jail, you will still be okay."

Even if.

Our worst-case scenarios can paralyze us. Death, jail, bankruptcy, chronic illness, sexual abuse, mental illness, unemployment, divorce, cancer—whatever you're fighting right now—can threaten your hope. It's normal to fear. It's tempting to wander in the wilderness of "what-ifs." But you can't camp out there forever if you want to survive.

Even if your worst fears come to pass—you will be okay. No matter the depths you've gone to, no matter the intensity of the fight, *even if* it doesn't turn out the way you've planned, dreamed, or hoped, faith says you'll be all right.

> *That's the difference between faith and fear. Fear wonders what if, but faith proclaims even if.*

You may think that Keith and Kass have faith because Keith didn't go to jail. But neither their faith nor yours is dependent on circumstance. It can't be. True faith is being confident in what we hope for and certain of what we can't see (Hebrews 11:1). God can do what we can't. *Even if* we can't see it.

He is who He says he is.

He keeps His promises.

His way is perfect.

He will never leave you.

He won't forsake you.

He is for you.

He sees you.

He is with you.

We have *this* hope as an anchor for our soul, and it's holding you, firmly and securely (Hebrews 6:19). And *even if*, He will be with you still.

Acknowledgements

Some book writers are authors first and speakers second. Others, consider themselves speakers first and authors second. I fall into the latter group because I really just want to talk about the book, not do the grueling work of writing it!

This is my struggle. But I've learned that if I wrestle words into submission on a page, eventually I'll get to talk out loud to real humans about them. That's what helps me press on when the writing gets hard.

Ask any of the people who've lived through the writing process with me, and they'd tell you that when I emerge from either a ten-hour writing day or a solitary writing retreat, it's hard to shut me up!

A book may seem like it's written by one person, but countless people behind the curtain truly make the magic happen. I'm profoundly grateful for those who contributed in meaningful ways to this one:

To my publishing team at Morgan James, especially my rockstar publisher and acquisitions editor, Karen Anderson. You get me, you get "it," and you love others well. Thank you for pushing me to rethink my concept and for taking my calls, even if you don't want to help me design another book cover over the phone! To David Hancock, our chief, who is accessible to his authors and has a genuine heart to see each of us succeed. And to Aubrey Kosa, my managing editor, I appreciate your detailed follow-through and the patience and care you showed me every step of this process.

To Susie Albert Miller, my precious friend and foreword writer, your wisdom top to bottom is astounding. Not only have you lived in hard places, but you also strive to encourage others in the midst of theirs. Your fortitude and faith are unparalleled. Thank you for your support. I'm honored to share a cover with you.

To my editors, Linda, Sissi, and Aubrey, an author is only as good as the editor who stands behind them. You made everything I wrote miles better.

To my early edition readers, Cassie, Nick, Dani, Craig, Stephanie, Susie, Barb, Robin, Candie, Patricia, Blair and Mallory. My readers might never see your input but every piece of feedback, large or small, improved this book.

To my experts and teachers, Stephanie Porter, Garrett Wilk, Susie Albert Miller, Byron Emmert, and my pastors, Dustin, Galen, and Kay Woodward, thank you for shining your light of wisdom in places I didn't understand. Whether you know it or not, your fingerprints are all over these pages. Thank you for the expertise you share with the world in each of your chosen professions.

To Cassie, my trusted traveling buddy, partner in crime, and "employee." You could never get paid enough for all you're worth to me. Thank you for the hours of behind-the-scenes research and hard work that helped me make my deadlines. Here's to more travel, book launches, and memories together in the future.

To Dawn, my friend for life, and my go-to for all things graphically beautiful. Thank you for the gorgeous front cover! Your talents are unending, and I'm overwhelmed by your generosity in always sharing them willingly with me. Love ya, man!

To Stephanie, I'm proud of all you've accomplished. Your knowledge and gems of insight benefit me every time we talk. Your assistance and editing brainstorm sessions in the eleventh hour were a saving grace! Can't wait to help you with *your* first book.

To Keith and Kassandra, with my gratitude for your confidence and trust in me. Your story changed this book, and I have learned so much from you both about how to love and persevere, no matter what life throws at you. Your friendship means the world to me.

To the countless, named and unnamed, people who bravely shared their hard places so that I could craft them into words that would benefit others, thank you. There is no book if people like you aren't willing to speak truth and life in dark places.

To my Copper Pointe Church family, especially my prayer team and my atrium dream team peeps. Y'all know who you are … know that your support didn't go unnoticed and I am grateful for the way you cheer for me.

To my people—my truth speakers, prayer warriors, believers-in-me—life is better because of you. Mom, Terry, Cassie, Dee, Heather, Dawn, Stephanie, Kay, and Pam, I cherish each of you. Thank you for coming alongside me.

To each of my children, I adore you, and I am blessed to call you some of my best friends in the world:

Nick, your early feedback for this manuscript was astute and helpful, and your grace in giving it even more. I am proud of the writer you're becoming and the way you've taken your gift of encouragement to the next level. At just the right moments you gave me fortitude, whether through a kind word or a timely prayer. Thank you for the beautiful headshots too. You know how to make even your old momma look pretty good.

Dani, my compatriot book lover, I pray you never lose your zeal for reading. Thank you for your valuable comments to improve the book. You can't know how much I loved every little smiley face, sweet comment, and exclamation point! Each one spurred me on. I cherish our friendship, your pride in me, and your love for life.

Mosey, you sacrificed more than the others because all this book writing (x2!) took place while you were still at home. I love that you are my cheerleader, my fan, and that you read my words—even if reading isn't your favorite. You show me love in many big and small ways, and I am going to cry my eyes out when you leave me next year for college.

To Craig, if I could, I'd dedicate every book I ever write to you because I couldn't do any of it without you. From picking up the slack at home, to caring for my every need, to showing up after hours to sit in the office next door silently working so I wouldn't be alone. You are my rock, my soul mate, and my best friend in the world. Thank you for showing me the forgiveness and love of Jesus, always. Grateful for every day we get to do life together.

To all the people who are facing hard places, thank you for shining your light, even when it feels dim. You matter, you are seen, and you are loved. I couldn't have written this book without your story in my heart. Keep pressing on in faith; God isn't finished with you yet.

And finally, my greatest debt is to Jesus, who saved me, remade me, and crafted me into something precious in His sight.

About the Author

Sarah Beckman inspires people from the stage and on the page. A sought-after national speaker and best-selling author of *Alongside: A Practical Guide for Loving Your Neighbor in Their Time of Trial,* she's passionate about helping people navigate the rough patches of life. Her own health and personal trials coupled with her experience walking alongside those facing all manner of hardship, provide her with an authentic, compelling viewpoint for her books.

Sarah has a B.A. in Journalism from the University of Wisconsin and is a seasoned media guest. Her TV appearances include *The 700 Club, The Difference with Matt and Kendal Hagee,* and *100 Huntley Street,* and she has recorded over fifty local and national radio programs and podcasts. She blogs at sarahbeckman.org and regularly contributes to many online and print publications.

Sarah thrives when she's coming alongside others in hard places. She serves at her local church and volunteers with several domestic and international non-profits. She and her husband Craig have been married for twenty-six years. They live in Albuquerque, New Mexico, and have three grown children.

Other Titles by Sarah Beckman:

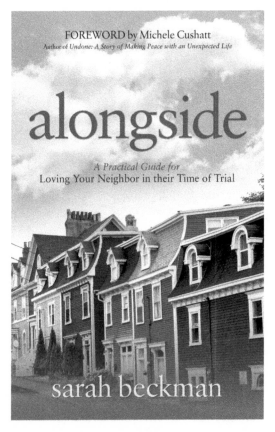

Alongside: A Practical Guide for Loving Your Neighbor in Their Time of Trial

Available wherever books are sold.

Let's Connect!

Find Sarah on social media:

Facebook: @sarahbeckman

Instagram: @sarahbeckmanauthor

Twitter: @sarahbeckman14

Book Sarah to speak to your group:

Email: speaking@sarahbeckman.org

Join the conversation:

Subscribe to Sarah's website to receive her updates and blog posts at www.sarahbeckman.org

Find Hope in your Hard Place:

Get your personalized scripture cards to encourage you at www.sarahbeckman.org/printable-scripture-cards

Discover hope in God's word with this curated list of scripture verses to help you find hope in your hard place at www.sarahbeckman.org/find-hope-verses

References

Chapter 3
Sproul, RC. *Now That's a Good Question*. Wheaton, Illinois: Tyndale House Publishers, Inc, 1996.

Chapter 11
Cloud, Henry and John Townsend. *Boundaries*. Grand Rapids, Michigan: Zondervan, 1992

Chapter 16
Voskamp, Ann. *One Thousand Gifts*. Grand Rapids, Michigan: Zondervan, 2010.